Here Rolled The Covered Wagons

HERE ROLLED THE COVERED WAGONS

by

Albert and Jane Salisbury

THIRD REVISED EDITION

BONANZA BOOKS · NEW YORK

This book is dedicated to

OLIVER MAXSON SALISBURY

FOREWORD

FOURTEEN years ago as a rookie traveling salesman I learned two sad truths that led to the creation of this book. As I paced the hotel room one Saturday afternoon, wondering if the day were going to last forever, my first disillusionment came. Those exotic adventures in which traveling men supposedly revel were dreamed up by the men themselves while they idled away lonely Saturdays and Sundays in a hotel room.

My two hobbies of photography and Northwest history came to my rescue. I remembered how as children my older sister and I listened to a Montana pioneer tell about the exciting early days; how we poked inquisitive fingers into bullet holes Indians had put in his log cabin during the Nez Perce War; how we peered for hours at yellowed newspapers that lined his walls. Then I thought of my father, Oliver M. Salisbury, a pioneer in picture making, who experimented with and talked about photography so much that I named my first rag doll 'Togaphy.

That gave me an idea of how to kill those tiresome weekends.

Sunday morning I set out to photograph a monument that had interested me during the week. As I neared the site, my second disillusionment came. There had been a snowstorm the week before but not one single track had broken the white surface around the monument. Of the thousands of people who had whizzed by on that heavily-traveled road, none had been interested enough to turn off the highway and pause a moment to read the monument's inscription. Yet this was a place where many men had died to make the West—the very land where the heedless travelers lived. What a thankless task had been that of the historical society which had spent time and money erecting a marker! Then and there the need for a book telling how to get to these places and why they were important became apparent.

Since that day nearly every place of historic interest in the Pacific Northwest has been visited and photographed. In a few cases the picture never seemed quite right and I requested permission from others to use their photographs. They are listed on the page of acknowledgments. The hundreds of sites and the thousands of pictures that were taken presented a problem. To describe them all would take several volumes. Limiting the choice to only the most important places was no answer, since opinions differ as to what is important.

The selection of material was finally based on three points. First, the accessibility to the highway on a regular tour route. Second, the interest in the historic episode that occurred there. Third, the possibility of securing good photographs on or near the spot.

My wife Jane, becoming more and more engrossed as we pored over the pictures and research books, wrote the text.

The purpose of the book is to create interest in the early Pacific Northwest, and to make available to those already interested the information necessary to enjoy these spots by the roadside that made history. With this in mind, we have selected as many places as possible over the six states involved.

The stories have been so arranged that a tour may be made, beginning at Yellowstone Park and following the course shown on the map at the book's end. An alternate route from Weiser, Idaho, to Seattle via Lewiston and Walla Walla appears on the map. Near each historic landmark a town has been selected as a convenient basing point. Directions from the basing point to the historic spot are given on the route which the authors consider best. If the reader wishes to peruse events in historical rather than geographical sequence, the chronological index makes this possible.

Seattle, Washington   Albert P. Salisbury

THIRD REVISED EDITION

In this Third Revised Edition, we have striven to give the reader a more complete picture of the early fur trade and the Oregon Trail by taking in new territory and adding the "Early St Louis and Manuel Lisa," and the "Fort Laramie" stories.

Other material that has been added is "The Death of Sgt. Floyd," to our way of thinking one of the most dramatic incidents of the Lewis and Clark Expedition, and the story of "Chief Sealth" for whom the city of Seattle was named.

Numerous photograph substitutions and changes have been made wherever we thought we could give the reader a better visualization of the early west.

Seattle, Washington   A. P. S.

CONTENTS

14

Here Rolled The Covered Wagons

COLTER'S HELL,
YELLOWSTONE PARK

[1]

EARLY IN the 1800's when John Colter described the boiling, churning, roaring phenomena of this region, those who listened were dubious. His tales of bubbling mud and spouting steam sounded like an imaginary hell to them, so they referred to it as "Colter's Hell." Without returning to civilized country after his two-year travels with the Lewis and Clark Expedition, Colter had discovered and explored this area while trading and trapping in the new West.

Jim Bridger, another adventurous mountain man of the early days, also examined the peculiar geographical freaks of Yellowstone. No man to fear hazards, Bridger could also spin a fine story. He told of a mountain of glass in Yellowstone so clear no one could see it. Another of his whimsies concerned a "peetrified forest with a peetrified bird sitting on a peetrified limb singing a peetrified song." Because Bridger's tall tales only intensified the disbelief which greeted his true yarns, they were all lumped under the heading "Bridger's Lies."

Except for sporadic explorations the solitude of this area was seldom broken. Although Indians occasionally came to the obsidian cliffs seeking material for arrowheads they generally avoided the region because of the extreme long winters and scarcity of animals. For the same reason trappers were not attracted to this country.

As more pioneers came West interest in the wonders of the region grew. In 1872 the area became Yellowstone National Park, the first region to be so reserved for the "enjoyment of all the people." The park's name came from the Yellowstone River where the rocks are coated with a yellowish silt.

Among those touring the park in 1877 was the Carpenter-Cowan party. Frank Carpenter, hoping to have a pleasant vacation seeing the geyser country, set out on horseback with a friend, Albert Oldham. At each stopping place along the way they found others anxious to join them in viewing the spectacle of Yellowstone. The party grew to include A. J. Arnold, Charles Mann, William Dingee, Ida Carpenter, George and Emma Cowan, Henry Meyers and the necessary conveyances. Mrs. Cowan and Ida were Carpenter's sisters.

17

INFERNO: Many men were called liars when they described phenomena such as this.

HELL ROARER: Sometimes it still is necessary to show photographs proving that steam roaring from the ground is a reality at Yellowstone.

After leisurely wandering through the park for several weeks they made night camp August 23 near the east fork of the Firehole River. They amused themselves during what was to be their last evening in the basin by singing, dancing and having what Carpenter later called a "grand jollification," quite unaware that a few Indians were watching them from the brush.

These were members of a Nez Perce band which was withdrawing toward Canada, occasionally engaging in battles with the pursuing United States Army. (See "Bear Paw Battle.")

The next morning three Indians entered the tourists' camp asking for bacon. flour and other foods.

The members of the party, after giving them some, broke camp hurriedly, keeping their weapons and scanty ammunition ready. Once out of the timber they saw a line of Indians and ponies extending three miles before them. The whites abandoned their wagons as the ransacking warriors milled around the party. Tension mounted as increasing hordes of Indians pushed into the group when they continued their trek. Dingee and Arnold escaped into the woods.

Suddenly an Indian opened fire and Cowan fell from his horse, shot in the head. Oldham, his face wounded, staggered into the brush to freedom. In the confusion of more shooting, shouting and jostling, Mann and Meyers fled. Leaving Cowan for dead, the Indians took prisoner Carpenter, Ida Carpenter and Emma Cowan.

The three were treated decently at the Indian camp where they spent the night. This raid, like others, was conducted because the Indians needed guns, ammunition, food and good horses; the Nez Perce chiefs ordinarily did not approve the wanton killing or kidnapping in which impetuous or vengeful tribesmen sometimes indulged. The prisoners realized, however, that they might be killed because they knew too much about the activities and location of the withdrawing Nez Perce.

The next day the Indians held council and freed them. Traveling on horseback until at last met by friends with a buggy, they went to Bozeman. However, their joy at release was dulled by sorrow for Cowan.

But George Cowan was alive. It was quiet when he regained consciousness. Thinking he was alone he crawled away in search of water. A nearby Indian noticed the movement and fired a shot that went through Cowan's hip and out his abdomen. As the Indian rode away Cowan lay waiting for death which he was sure would come to him as he thought it had to his wife and friends. When he realized he was going to live, he dragged his partially paralyzed body the nine miles back to the looted wagon. It took him 60 hours. Finding no food he crawled another four miles to a former camp where he found some coffee grounds. He made a pot of coffee, his first food in five days. The next day scouts from General O. O. Howard's command found the emaciated man. Arnold was with the troops who carried Cowan away in a jolting wagon. Although Arnold carefully nursed his friend, the three-week trip to a ranch 40 miles from Bozeman was agonizing. During the journey Cowan's recovery was spurred when he learned through a soldier that his wife was alive. Emma Cowan, reading of her husband's escape from death in a newspaper account of General Howard's report, met him at the ranch where he rested several days before going on to Bozeman.

The final fillip to his string of afflictions came to Cowan in a Bozeman hotel. As his wounds were being dressed one evening the bedstead broke down. The undaunted Cowan looked up at his friends from the floor and suggested they'd better get out the artillery if they couldn't kill him any other way.

TOP OF THE WORLD

GRAND CANYON

TRAPPERS' RENDEZVOUS, JACKSON'S HOLE, WYOMING

[2] Basing point: Yellowstone Lake, Wyoming. Take U. S. Highway 89, 23 mi. to Snake River, the southern park entrance. Continue on same highway 20 mi. to Moran. Most of the distance Jackson Lake can be seen to the right.

Enter Grand Teton National Park just a few miles south of Snake River. You will pass Jackson and Jenny lakes, and leave the park at Jackson.

Synthetic cowboys abound here, both summer and winter, thanks to the numerous dude ranches. Jackson's Hole country is noted for its winter sports as well as for its summer vacation facilities.

HERE INDIANS hunted for many decades before the white man made it a fur rendezvous.

John Colter, the first white man to visit this country, was followed by Jim Bridger, Captain Bonneville and other noted trail blazers. The "pilot knobs," as the Tetons at Jackson's Hole were called, were pointed out to Wilson Price Hunt by Edward Robinson, who told Hunt that there lay the headwaters of the Snake River. The section was named after David Jackson, of the firm of Jackson, Sublette and Jedediah Smith.

As more people passed through this region, it expanded into one of the largest fur rendezvous. Traders came from Montana, Wyoming, Idaho, Utah, Oregon and Washington. The rendezvous system involved a large campground where, at certain specified times, hunters and trappers assembled to turn over their catch to the companies. The companies sent out wagons or pack trains loaded with provisions for the trappers as well as baubles for trading purposes. This plan saved the fur companies the expense of maintaining permanent outposts.

Liquor for Indians was forbidden by law, with slight effect. The Indian hunters and white trappers wanted entertainment, which the companies frequently supplied in liquid form. As the men grew merrier the price of their furs dropped, until at times they had nothing but a headache in payment for a rich catch.

The fur companies likewise had their problems. The costly pack trains might be waylaid by thieves. Also, heavy competition between the companies was not always as clean as it was keen, and rival outfits constantly struggled to get the upper hand by any means.

Beaver, buffalo, otter and mink pelts changed hands in the surging throng at rendezvous time. It was an exciting break in the lonely lives of the fur men, even if some came away empty-handed. In those high days of the fur trade there was always another year to trap, always more animals to snare for the next rendezvous.

22

THE PILOT KNOBS: The Three Tetons served as landmarks in the early days for travelers going both east and west.

JACKSON'S HOLE
Seen from the pass on the Wyoming-Idaho state line.

FORT HENRY, FIRST WHITE HABITATION WEST OF THE ROCKIES

[3] Basing point: St. Anthony, Idaho. From the center of town, go north on U. S. Highway 191 to Second Street. Turn left on good oiled road 4 mi. to Parker, a small community. After crossing railroad tracks in the center of town, continue south 1 block. Turn right on good oiled road, continue south 1 mi. where a gravel road cuts in from the left (south). Go down this road 1.9 mi. to Henry's Fork Bridge. Continue 0.2 mi. to the first gate on left after crossing the bridge. Leave car here. Go through gate and follow old road 675 paces east. The monument marking the site of old Fort Henry is on a slight rise of ground in the open above the river bottom.

Nature is lavish and man is frugal in this sugar beet country. The productive acres are farmed generally by Mormons, who live in unpretentious, neat houses. What looks like the ruins of a feudal castle at the left of the road is actually part of an obsolete sugar beet factory.

THE QUEST for furs built Fort Henry, and snows defeated it.

The principal fur companies operating in the northwest, other than the British posts, were the Missouri, the Rocky Mountain and the American Fur companies.

In 1808 Manuel Lisa, founder of the Missouri Company, returned to Missouri from the fort bearing his name on the Yellowstone, at the mouth of the Big Horn River. Exhibiting his fair catch of furs, he was able to interest Andrew Henry in his company. Lisa sent Henry and a man named Menard guided by the incredible John Colter, to build a fort on the three forks of the Missouri River in the spring of 1810. The rancor of the Blackfeet Indians prevented trapping. Henry was robbed, and several of his trappers killed.

Searching for safer trapping grounds, Henry and a small party of men crossed the Continental Divide and discovered the north fork of the Snake River, later known as Henry's Fork. They explored the region and built several log cabins and a dugout. Even though beaver skins were obtainable and the Indians did not bother them, the severe winter proved this site unwise. There was little edible game available. In the stinging cold of that winter they killed their horses for food. In the spring of 1811 Henry and his dispirited men returned across the Divide to Three Forks. Finding the post deserted, they went on down the Yellowstone.

At Fort Henry, Wilson Price Hunt and his Astorians, in October of 1811, built the 15 cottonwood canoes in which they attempted to navigate the Snake River.

After this episode, the site of the fort was unknown for nearly 100 years. A century later a rock was unearthed bearing the words "Al the cook, but nothing to cook." Later two other rocks were discovered, one reading "Govt. Camp 1811," and the other "Fort Henry 1811 by Capt. Hunt."

SILENT BECKONING: The Tetons as Henry and his men viewed them from the west side.

NO BLACKFEET, NO BEAVER, NO BISCUITS: The long-lost site of Fort Henry. The two cabins and dirt cellar on this spot protected against snow but not against hunger.

FORT HALL AND THE OREGON TRAIL

[4] Basing point: Blackfoot or Pocatello, Idaho. From Blackfoot take Highway 91, 13 mi. south to Fort Hall and Monument.

To see traces of Old Oregon Trail turn back (north) 0.3 mi. from the monument. Turn right across railroad tracks and go back along tracks on east side 0.3 mi. Turn left on gravel road. Go 2.6 mi. Here part way up the hill is a lonesome cemetery to the left. Traces of the Oregon Trail are still clearly visible between the road and the cemetery.

To reach the actual location of Old Fort Hall, go 0.3 mi. north from the monument on the main highway. Here take gravel road to left. The distance is 6 or 7 mi., the road poor and, in the river bottoms, confusing. Secure permission at the Fort Hall Indian Agency, as well as directions, for the site is difficult to locate.

If you knock on a door along this road, don't be surprised to see a cow peer out at you. Most of the road is in the Fort Hall Indian Reservation. Although provided with neat houses by the government, some of the Bannack and Shoshone Indians feel more at home in tepees and stable their stock in the houses.

The road to Oregon came through the Divide from Soda Springs to Mount Putnam. Descending a long hill, it then cut across the dry sagebrush-covered flats to Fort Hall.

Later this same route was followed by cattlemen driving their prime steers to market. Legend has it that one herd bedded down in the gap for the night. Frightened somehow, they stampeded pell-mell toward the flats, trampling hundreds of their number underfoot as they crowded down the narrow ravine.

WHEN THE Rocky Mountain Fur Company broke its fur-buying contract with Nathaniel J. Wyeth, he found himself out in the wilds with no place to store his goods. ". . . Found a location for a Fort . . . ," reads the July 14, 1834, entry in *Journal of Nathaniel J. Wyeth*. "July fifteenth commenced building. . . ." He needed storage space. From this simple beginning developed Fort Hall, destined to become an extremely important point on the Oregon Trail.

Building material was plentiful. Close by was a cottonwood forest, and his men found abundant well-seasoned driftwood in the Snake River. The original fort was upright cottonwood logs. The stockade was about 15 feet high and 80 feet square. Two bastions stood at diagonal corners.

At Fort Hall, the Reverend Jason Lee, tall, powerful Methodist missionary, delivered on July 27 what was almost certainly the first sermon preached in Idaho. Lee was popular with the rough mountain men. His sermon, although well received that morning, did not deter the men from their afternoon's horse-racing. A Frenchman named Kanseau was thrown from his horse and killed. The next day Jason Lee delivered what was probably another first in Idaho: the funeral service of Mr. Kanseau. The body was sewn in buffalo robes and buried 150 yards south of the fort.

CROSSROADS OF THE WEST

The site of Fort Hall in the Snake River bottom. *Right:* Scars left by wagon trains on the hills above Fort Hall.

Raising of a home-made American flag signified the completion of Fort Hall on August 5, 1834. The flag was fashioned of red flannel, unbleached sheeting and blue cloth.

Liquor was served following the flag-raising ceremony. ". . . The consequence was a scene of rioting, noise and fighting during the whole day. . . ," according to J. K. Townsend, a member of the party. "We had gouging, biting, fistcuffing and stomping in the most scientific perfection; some even fired guns and pistols at each other, but the weapons were mostly harmless in the unsteady hands that employed them."

Wyeth sold Fort Hall to the Hudson's Bay Company in 1837.

Located in rich fur country and at the intersection of Indian trails, the fort became the rendezvous of such famous mountain men as Jim Bridger, Joe Meek, Kit Carson and others. Indians also flocked to the fort to trade. Here the Oregon Trail emigrants stopped to repair their wagons, rest their stock and all too often die of cholera or typhoid contracted on the way. 1,288 miles from Independence and with the next stop, Fort Boise, 300 miles to the west, Fort Hall assumed great prominence on the Trail.

Abandoned with the advent of the railroads, the exact site of the fort was unknown for years. Ezra Meeker, on his trip retracing the Old Oregon Trail, rediscovered it in 1916. All that remains is a faint outline of the fort's foundations.

MOUNT PUTNAM: Landmark on the Oregon Trail with the ruts of the old road showing clearly in the foreground.

SPRING CREEK FORD: As the immigrant trail neared Fort Hall, there were many such streams to be forded. The ruts cut deep by the wagon wheels show on the far side of the creek.

THE OREGON TRAIL

THE OREGON TRAIL was literally beaten into the ground by the iron rims of countless wagon wheels. In some prairie stretches it sprawled 20 miles wide. Where mountains or other obstructions caused the road to converge, the wagon wheels, aided by wind and storm, pounded ruts four to seven feet deep into the ground.

The Trail followed old Indian and buffalo paths along the rivers and through mountain passes. In 1805 Lewis and Clark had used the same route along the Missouri and Columbia rivers. Perhaps the first men to use South Pass were the mountain men and fur traders of the Missouri Fur Company.

Robert Stuart and a party of Astorians followed the general course of the Trail in 1812. Between 1832 and 1836 the parties of Nathaniel Wyeth and Captain Benjamin Bonneville journeyed the perilous 2020 miles from Independence, Missouri, to Astoria, Oregon.

The real migration commenced in 1842, continuing until the completion of the railroads in the 1870's. During this period it is estimated that over 200,000 people traversed this Great Medicine Road of the Whites, as the Indians called it.

Much of the trail was desert land. Pioneer diaries described it as littered with handsome furniture, heavy stoves and feather beds, all found too burdensome for the long journey. Farther along the Trail wagons were abandoned after teams died for lack of grass. Carcasses of horses, cattle and oxen strewed the wayside.

Hundreds of the pioneers died of cholera, or at the hands of enemy Indians. After a roadside burial it was customary to drive the wagons over the graves, obliterating them to keep wolves or Indians from disinterring the remains. The custom was not always followed; graves were frequently seen with headstones of rough rock, hand-hewn pine or simple stakes. Roberta Frye Watt tells in *Four Wagons West* of a pioneer woman seeing such a grave, a very tiny one with a pink sunbonnet on it.

29

THE LITTLE SPRING
CREEK MURDER

[5] Basing point: Pocatello, Idaho. Take U. S. Highway 30N, 79 mi. east and south to the town of Soda Springs. To reach Little Spring Creek continue on main highway 1 mi. east of the county courthouse in the center of town. The overpass crosses Little Spring Creek. The Wagon Box Grave is in the city cemetery, 1 block west of the courthouse and 1 block north. The easily located grave is on the west side of the cemetery.

Although the people of Soda Springs practically live on the Oregon Trail, they know little of its background. After five or six inquiries someone finally remembered where Little Spring Creek was. The Soda Springs themselves have historic interest and quite graphic names. One which must have tasted pretty good to a long-ago trail blazer was named Beer Springs. Another, Antipolygamy Springs, was thought to have cooled the men's romantic ardor.

SOMETIMES DEATH was the destiny of pioneers seeking a new life in the West.

One morning a wagon train pulled away from Little Spring Creek, where it had camped overnight. One family stayed behind. The father of the family explained that his horses were lost and he would not continue without them.

The next morning three men saw the lone wagon standing by Little Spring Creek. Curious, the men, George Goodhart, Bill Wilburn and John Taung, went to investigate. They found the father, mother and five children had been murdered.

"They had made their beds on the ground by their wagon," George Goodhart later told Abraham C. Anderson. "I think the murderers came up when they were sound asleep and killed the father. It looked like the mother had grabbed the baby and started to run. I think her screams woke the children. She was found dead with her feet on the bed and her body on the ground, her baby in her arms. The oldest boy was about a rod from the wagon. The next oldest boy was around behind the wagon . . . with a broken arrow in his back . . . The girl was lying about three feet from her mother at the foot of the bed . . . The boy next to the baby was in bed with his throat cut . . . The mother was stabbed in the breast. It looked like the baby had been stabbed above the ear . . . It may have been done for revenge.

"I think the Indians had stolen his horses and had them cached . . . the emigrants told us that the man was very brave. I think that when he found the horses cached he must have taken a shot at the Indians and taken his horses by force. And the Indians followed them up and murdered them while all were asleep."

Goodhart and his party took the bodies to the place of burial and dug a grave. They laid the father and mother side by side, the baby in its mother's arms, and the rest of the children around their parents in the same wagon box that the family had lived and traveled in for so many miles to the lonely knoll at Soda Springs.

30

LOOKING BACKWARD: To the east of Little Spring Creek, the Oregon Trail came through sagebrush that is now a wheatfield.

JOURNEY'S END: No longer a lonely grave but a permanent memorial to the pioneer family and the poor spelling of the monument maker.

MASSACRE ROCKS AND ROCK CREEK CAMP

[6] Basing point: American Falls, Idaho. Take U. S. Highway 30N, 11.1 mi. west. Or come east from Rupert 38 mi. The rocks are marked by a monument on the east side. They can be easily recognized, as the road runs through a narrow defile once known as the Gate of Death.

Rock Creek Camp is 1 mi. east on the same highway. The bridge across Rock Creek is the first after passing Massacre Rocks. The campsite is on the south side of the road.

History lovers won't like what has been done to Rock Creek Camp. Formerly barren and utterly lonely, with a poignant pull at the imagination, the camp has been converted into a conventional little park.

GATE OF DEATH, Devil's Gate, Massacre Gate and Massacre Rocks were the names given this obstacle on the Oregon Trail, and it lived up to them all.

The opening in the rocks was narrow, but avoiding the rocks entirely involved considerable extra travel, extremely arduous to those Oregon Trail pioneers. Chancing the small opening meant the possibility of encountering enemy Indians who found the rocks excellent hiding places. The Oregon Trailers took the chance.

The first known incident occurred in 1851. A group of emigrants, led by a Virginian named Miller, approached the rocks. Indians hidden among the boulders attacked them. One man was killed and one of Miller's girls wounded, but the party escaped through the Gate of Death.

Later that same year Hudson Clark and his family from Illinois were assailed. Traveling in a light wagon somewhat ahead of the main train, the Clarks were allowed to go through the gap. As they emerged the Indians attacked them, killing Clark's mother and brother. His sister was wounded, dragged from the wagon and raped.

Still later in 1851 a wagon train led by a man named Harpool fought a two-hour battle with Indians at the opening before repulsing them.

A large train of 52 wagons carrying 88 men and 46 women drew near Massacre Rocks on August 10, 1862. The train was divided into three sections. Snake Indians concealed among the rocks permitted one section to pass. The second section was attacked as it went through the defile. One man was killed and a woman shot in the neck. The horses were run off and the wagons pillaged. Feather beds were ripped open and the bloody feathers strewn on the ground, the wind blowing them around to add to the confusion of the scene.

Simultaneously, the first section four miles farther on suffered a like fate. Two men were killed, several wounded, but most of the livestock were saved.

The third and last section of the train had made noon camp some miles back on the trail. Warned of the attack by a messenger from the second section, it moved up.

GATE OF DEATH: Massacre Rocks from the west. The old road came through the gap following the same course as the present highway.

PLACE OF REST: A favorite campsite of the emigrants. Here they rested and repaired their wagons. For many it was a final resting place.

"We . . . found quite a quantity of blood, and fragments of such things as immigrants usually carry with them," wrote John C. Hilman, a member of the party. "It was evident that the Indians had done their hellish deeds in a hasty manner and left . . . We were obliged to camp on the very ground which the Indians had a few hours previous, made to ring with their pandemonium-like shouts, and red with the blood of innocent men and women . . . We hoped the night would be a short one."

The following day an expedition was organized to attempt the recovery of the stolen stock. Ezra Meeker once asserted that the slogan "Keep cool" helped carry families safely over the Trail. It was not always easy to keep cool. When the expedition encountered Indians, one of the emigrants, angered by the events of the preceding day, fired on them. The Indians immediately attacked. Outnumbered, the emigrants defended themselves as best they could in a running battle of three miles. Three men were killed and scalped and several wounded before the Indians gave up the chase.

In the three attacks George Adams, George Shepard, A. J. Winter, Charles Bullwinkle, William Motes, Thomas Newman, Maesmo Lepi and an unidentified Italian were killed. Elizabeth Adams died of her wounds.

All the victims were buried along the Trail. Adams, Shepard, Winter, Bullwinkle and Lepi were interred side by side, the Italian at the rocks and Elizabeth Adams at Raft River, a few miles farther on.

WHOSE WAS HE? WHO WERE HIS?

STONE TABLET: The camp register at Rock Creek is covered with the names of people long gone from this spot and long gone from this world. Yet the names are as clearly engraved on this rock as the deeds of the signers are engraved in history.

PIONEER BOY'S SLATE

Apparently he returned at the age of 49 to admire his boyhood handiwork.

THE CALIFORNIA CUT-OFF AT RAFT RIVER

[7] Basing point: American Falls, Idaho. On U. S. Highway 30, drive 24 mi. east of American Falls, or 14 mi. east of Massacre Rocks.

Only coyotes and jack rabbits tolerate this bleak sagebrush country. The green growth along Raft River is a reviving sight to the speeding wayfarer of today. How doubly welcome it must have been to the emigrants in their ox-drawn wagons.

ALTHOUGH the Raft River country was rich in wild game and fur-bearing animals, the river itself was formidable to the trappers and emigrants. It was considerably larger than it is today. Fording was the usual method of traversing this beaver-dam-choked river, but the stream probably derived its name from some party crossing it on a raft.

Peter Skene Ogden of the Hudson's Bay Company was familiar with the Raft River country. His successor, John Work, wrote in his journal of a trapping expedition to the river in 1831, during which he shot buffalo from several herds.

The noted trapper and guide Milton Sublette led Nathaniel Wyeth, founder of Fort Hall, up the Raft River in 1832. With Sublette were his Indian wife, three-year old child, and their baby who was born on the journey. The three-year-old, tied on a gentle horse, followed the party with the herd of horses.

The influx of emigrants along the Oregon Trail made the Raft River territory with its lush grass a refreshing stopover. There the tired oxen recuperated for the trials ahead.

The Raft River turnoff, four or five miles south of its mouth, became a division point for wagon trains. Those going to Washington and Oregon crossed the river, continuing west along the Snake to Fort Boise and beyond. The California-bound parties also crossed the Raft River, but cut south up the river's west bank to join the Hudspeth Cut-off, passing through the City of Rocks and on to California.

Forerunners of the California Chamber of Commerce were stationed at various splits in the trail where a pioneer must decide whether to go north or south. At the Raft River turnoff one of those eager persuaders held forth, acquainting the emigrants with the dreadful dangers of Washington and Oregon territories as compared to the ease and plenty of California.

STORMS AHEAD

Californians to the contrary, it sometimes at least threatened to storm on the road south.

THE SILENT CITY OF ROCKS

[8] Basing point: Burley, Idaho. Turn left (south) in Burley, 24 mi. to Oakley. Turn left (east) on gravel road 1 mi. Here turn right (south) 12 mi. at junction with gravel road, turn east. The Silent City of Rocks, covering an area of 25 square miles, can be seen for 5 or 6 miles beyond this junction, mostly on the north side of the road.

Here it is easy to envisage the pioneers making camp, the oxen thirstily drinking from the brook, the released children shouting and playing, the diligent women cooking for their families.

The old names and dates, written so long ago with axle grease which the pioneers called wagon dope, are still clearly readable. Wind erosion has left the dope-protected letters standing in relief.

THE SILENT CITY OF ROCKS, as early wayfarers called this land, once rang with pioneer voices and resounded with cries of terror.

The California-bound Oregon Trailers, using the Hudspeth Cut-off, found this high mountain meadow a satisfactory stopover point. Since water was always a problem on the Trail, the Silent City with a stream running through it became a popular place to camp. Adventurers, explorers and emigrants rested here, repairing wagons while the women cooked and performed other chores. Horses and oxen, facing the strenuous pull through the mountains to California, restored their strength.

The pioneers often wrote names and dates on the rocks with wagon dope. Messages for people who were to follow were smeared on these natural tablets.

Erosion shaped the rocks into many weird formations which the emigrants named accordingly. At the Twin Sisters Rocks, in 1863, a group of seven wagons of returning Californians were attacked by Indians. Chief Pocatello and his Bannack warriors tomahawked and clubbed to death every man, woman and child in the party. Looting and burning the wagons, they drove off the stock.

The Silent City of Rocks stage station was three miles east of the Silent City proper. When a Kelton-to-Boise stage was held up, legend has it that $90,000 in gold was taken. One of the robbers was killed. The other, dying in prison, claimed he had hidden the gold near a clump of trees in the Silent City. Eager searchers have never found the gold.

BRIGHT HORIZON: The road to California from the Silent City of Rocks follows the old California cut-off.

EMBOSSED BY WIND

Written with wagon dope and embossed by the winds and storms of nearly a hundred years, these names are more permanent than the hands that wrote them.

BURIED TREASURE: View of the Silent City from one of its numerous caves.

THE ROAD THEY CAME BY: The old road from Almo Creek came through
the gap at the right.

PLAYFUL DRAGON: One of the weird spectacles at the Silent City of Rocks.

THE MASSACRE AT ALMO

[9] Basing point: See Silent City of Rocks. From junction of gravel roads at the Silent City of Rocks continue 9 mi. over gravel road to the village of Almo.

Going through the gap on the east side of the Silent City of Rocks, the road follows the route of the Hudspeth Cut-off from the Oregon Trail. Through the sagebrush, vestiges of the Trail can be seen.

This trip from the Silent City to Almo, which today takes 20 minutes, meant a full day of laborious travel to the Oregon Trailer.

A LARGE, well-equipped wagon train bedded down on Almo Creek one night in the summer of 1861. Although the usual precautions of corralling the wagons and posting armed guards were observed, the members felt secure. The large party of 60 wagons and 300 people had held off hostile Indians all the way from Missouri. Success added to their confidence.

Indians, angered by shots fired at them by the emigrants, felt increased enmity to the white men for their encroachment on Indian territory and at the same time coveted their wagons' contents. As the wagons rolled across southern Idaho, the red men began to appear in increasing numbers, called together from miles around by runners and signal fires. Gathering at Indian Grove, a timbered hill south of Almo Creek, they carefully laid their plans.

ON TO CALIFORNIA: The Hudspeth Cut-off followed by California-bound Oregon Trailers.

The monument reads:

ALMO IDAHO
DEDICATED TO THE MEMORY
OF THOSE WHO LOST THEIR LIVES IN A MOST
HORRIBLE INDIAN MASSACRE 1861
THREE HUNDRED IMMIGRANTS WEST BOUND
ONLY FIVE ESCAPED.
ERECTED BY S.& D. OF IDAHO PIONEERS
1938

EMBOSSED BY SUNLIGHT

In the morning the last wagon of the long train had left the creek and was moving in a cloud of yellow dust stirred up by the leaders when the Indians attacked. The wagon master immediately gave orders to corral the wagons with the stock inside.

The Indians had the advantage of the wagon party, despite their scarcity of arms. Their ability to conceal themselves behind any kind of cover and their overwhelming numbers enabled them to kill anyone who attempted to go for water or escape. As the original Indians tired, they returned to the grove and were replaced by others.

Lack of water made the situation desperate as the siege went on day and night. Feverishly the encircled emigrants dug a well, but to no avail. Thirst and the firing and whoops of the Indians stampeded the stock. In their terror they imperiled the lives of the people in the enclosure, and it was necessary to release them on the third day. The thirsty stock, heading for water, were promptly taken over by the Indians.

All in the enclosure knew what the end would be. During the fourth night a young man and woman escaped. Crawling through the sagebrush, they made their way to a settlement at Brigham, Utah. That same night another man, two women and a nursing baby made their escape. Creeping along on hands and knees, the mother carried her baby by clamping its garments in her teeth. They lived on roots and rose hips until found by a rescue party from Brigham.

Arriving at Almo Creek, the rescue party found that the remainder of the original party of 300 men, women and children had been overwhelmed by the Indians. Not one survived. The bodies were gathered and buried in the well they had so futilely dug.

A few days later a band of Indian braves, displaying scalps of white people on the manes and bridles of their horses, paraded through a white settlement.

THE WELL GRAVE: The last hope of the thirsty emigrant party was dug near the haystacks. The land is now well irrigated.

44

OLD EVEN WHEN NEW: A natural route through the Rockies for Indians and buffalo, when the white man came he called it from the very beginning the *Old* Oregon Trail.

MARCUS WHITMAN AND HIS WAGON

[10] Basing point: Buhl, Idaho. On U. S. Highway 30, go 22 mi. west to the village of Haberman. 0.5 mi. west of Haberman is the Oregon Trail monument commemorating Marcus Whitman and his party.

To the north of the Snake River, 10 mi. from Buhl, are the Thousand Springs. Early emigrants thought them of miraculous origin. It is now believed these mysterious springs are the outlet of Lost River, which sinks into the lava and disappears 150 mi. to the north.

NARCISSA PRENTICE WHITMAN was a woman with patience, courage, and a strong-willed husband to try them both.

In the spring of 1836 Marcus Whitman, his bride Narcissa, the Reverend and Mrs. Henry Harmon Spalding and a layman, William H. Gray, were sent by the American Board of Missions to establish a mission among the Nez Perce Indians.

Whitman was familiar with the country, having been in the Oregon territory the year before with the Reverend Samuel Parker. The missionaries crossed the plains with an American Fur Company expedition. The Oregon Trail, as yet unbroken by wagons, in some places consisted of only a narrow, steep and dangerous trail. The American Fur group cautiously abandoned their wagons at Fort Laramie.

Against the advice of almost the entire party, including his bride, Whitman determined to force his wagon on through to the Columbia.

In her many letters and her diary, Narcissa Whitman evidenced very little difference of opinion between herself and her husband. Regarding his efforts to take the wagon over the hazardous Trail, however, she wrote, "Husband had a tedious time with the wagon today. It got stuck in the creek . . . on the side of one [mountain] so steep it was difficult for the horses to pass, it upset twice . . . Ma knows what my feelings are."

Miles Goodyear, a 16-year-old boy whom Whitman had picked up in Missouri, refused to contend further with the handicap of the wagon and remained at Fort Hall. Whitman continued; his was the first wagon to persist that far on the Trail.

Misfortune and the wagon were traveling companions. "One of the axle trees of the wagon broke today," Narcissa wrote on July 28, 1836, "was a little rejoiced for we were in hopes they would leave it." But her persevering husband made a cart of the back wheels and lashed the front wheels to it. The grim Trail at last won its battle with the wagon, which Whitman left at Fort Boise.

Pushing on, Whitman and his party ultimately established a mission at Waiilatpu on the Columbia River. After the massacre (see "Whitman Massacre at Waiilatpu"), Dr. and Mrs. Whitman and the other slain were buried in a wagon box.

46

WAGONS MADE THE WEST: Marcus Whitman passed this way, toiling ceaselessly with his wagon.

THE WEST UNMADE THE WAGONS: The scarred sagebrush and deep ruts along this part of the Old Oregon Trail still give evidence of the thousands of Studebaker and Conestoga wagons that passed this way a century ago.

THREE ISLAND CROSSING

[11] Basing point: Glenn's Ferry, Idaho. On U. S. Highway 30, go 2 mi. west of Glenn's Ferry. The monument is on the north side of the road. The three islands can be seen in the Snake River on the south side.
Cattle and sheep flourish in this country, one of the greatest livestock ranges in the state.

HEAT, dust and thirst pursued the Oregon Trailers over the rough, barren country from the Raft River to the Snake.

After the Snake River was reached, the walls of the canyon were so steep in many places that the coveted water, plainly seen, was inaccessible. When the river did become accessible, it sometimes meant tragedy to the pioneers. Frequently the stock would stampede for the water.

"While watering, some of their cattle swam over the river," said Mrs. Elizabeth Smith, describing the situation as it happened to her party September 7, 1847. "One of the men swam after them but before he got across sank to rise no more. He left a wife and three children . . . the man that owned the cattle, however, took the horse and swam after them and while coming back . . . got off the horse and sank and was seen no more. He left a wife and six children. It is supposed there is a whirlpool at the bottom of the river."

The emigrants had to cross to the north side of the river at Three Island Crossing, or Island Ford. Always a dangerous crossing, it was sometimes essential to block the wagon beds and float them over. At times enemy Indians lay in wait and ambushed the pioneers as they crossed. Later a ferry was established.

Bannack Indian Chief Buffalo Horn and his band of 200 warriors raided Glenn's Ferry on June 2, 1878. Commandeering the ferry, they maneuvered themselves and their horses across the river. On the other side, the Indians plundered several wagonloads of merchandise which were waiting to cross. Finding quantities of liquor in one of the wagons, the hostiles staged a wild orgy all that night on the river banks.

Moving on down the river the next morning the Indians met John Bascom and two other men. Killing all three and taking their horses, the warriors proceeded farther along the river for more depradations.

DANGEROUS CROSSING: The wagons were "rough locked" so the wheels wouldn't turn, then skidded down this steep hill to the Three Island Crossing of the Snake River. To ford the river the teams were fastened together, the weakest in the middle. A single horseman, carrying one end of a rope, swam across to the first island. Guided by the rope, others on horseback followed until enough were across to pull the teams over. The process was repeated on each island until the **north bank was reached.**

GOLD RUSH VIOLENCE
AT IDAHO CITY

[12] Basing point: Boise, Idaho. From Boise take Idaho State Highway 21 south and east 45 mi. over good oiled road to Idaho City.

Boise itself has an interesting history. Early French fur company *voyageurs* named the river near Boise, Le Bois, or The Woods. The name was taken by the fort west of the present city, and finally the town assumed the name Boise City. Boise has a large Basque community.

Famed Arrow Rock Dam is on this stretch of road between Boise and Idaho City.

A LUSTY, roaring mining camp ruled by guns and gold, Idaho City was in 1863 the most important of the several placer mining spots in the Boise Basin.

Living was exciting, but always tentative for the city's 20,000 miners, gamblers, dance-hall girls, teamsters, tradesmen and the few miners' wives.

The rich gravel made rich men. Wealth wrested from the gulch was tossed away at the gaming tables or lost at the point of a road agent's pistol. The cemetery bears mute evidence of violence. Of the 200 graves dug there in 1863, only 28 were for people who died of natural causes.

Most of the notorious miscreants of the 1860's tried their luck at Idaho City. Gunman Cherokee Bob, road agent Henry Plummer, and the disreputable gambler Ferd Patterson were among those who pursued fortune in the turbulent town.

Patterson, who once had scalped alive an ex-mistress, was a garish exhibitionist, wearing a long, otter-trimmed coat, plaid trousers, a heavy gold-nugget watch chain and luxurious silk vest. An ardent, abusive Secessionist, he had murdered a river-boat captain who disagreed with him on the question of withdrawal from the Union.

Sheriff Pinkham of Idaho City also argued with Patterson on the same subject. The gambler shot him dead. The furious camp miners attempted to lynch Patterson. They were frustrated by the deputy sheriff who locked the gambler in the jail, which was inside a stockade. Through a hole in the stockade, the deputy threatened the mob with a cannon.

The first jail in Idaho, it was sturdy, perhaps because it wasn't used enough. It held Patterson until his trial when he was acquitted to the disgust of the cannoneer-deputy.

BAD MEN BEWARE: The first jail in Idaho was built at Idaho City.

CELL BLOCK: Where many desperadoes including Ferd Patterson were locked.

RICH GRAVEL MADE RICH MEN: The diggings at Idaho City.

THE LIVING PAST: Idaho City as it is today. Apparently its wealth was not used in maintenance.

FIRST MASONIC TEMPLE IN IDAHO

GOVERNMENT ISLAND

[13] Basing point: Boise, Idaho. Take U. S. Highway 20 west to Boise River bridge at city limits. Government Island can be seen in the river on the right side of the bridge.

Boise has a wealth of historic places. The Idaho State's Historical Society Museum in the Capitol Building is well worth seeing. The Coston cabin and Pearce cabin in Julia Davis Park were built in 1863. The O'Farrell cabin at 6th and Fort streets was also built in '63. An old stone blockhouse used as a refuge from Indian attacks is on the south side of the river near the Holcomb School.

WORKING WITH a gun in one hand and a trap in the other, the fur-seekers at Government Island reaped a heavy crop of pelts.

Wilson Price Hunt, exploring the Boise River in 1811, searched for suitable spots to establish trading posts. As the success of the fur trade depended largely on good relations with the Indians, Hunt held several peace conferences. The results of such conferences were always tenuous. The Wilson Price Hunt expedition failed.

The Boise River country, always a rich fur region, attracted Donald McKenzie of the North West Fur Company. His attempts to reopen the lands for trapping and trading were resisted by the Snake Indians.

"There is much danger and anxiety," observed Alexander Ross, one of McKenzie's party, ". . . for as an enemy is often lurking about, the hunter has to keep constant look out . . . Often one-half of the men set the traps and the other half keep guard over them."

Discovering a Snake Indian camp about where Boise now stands, McKenzie set up headquarters on Government Island. Several days' council with the Indian chiefs, the discussion seesawing back and forth, led at last to an amicable agreement. The amity lasted until the Indians became angered and alarmed by the increasing flow of emigrants over the Oregon Trail.

Besides being a favorable place to ford the river, Government Island was a popular campground on the Oregon Trail. John C. Fremont and his exploring party camped on the island in 1843.

54

BOISE'S BOYS

They now play Indian on Government Island in the Boise River.

GOVERNMENT ISLAND
ON THE RIGHT EXTENSIVELY USED
AS A CAMP BY PIONEERS OF
OREGON TRAIL

ERECTED BY PIONEER CHAPTER
D. A. R. 1932

THE ANNIHILATION OF
THE WARD WAGON TRAIN

[14] Basing point: Caldwell, Idaho. Take Highway 30 east to city limits. Turn right at sign pointing to Municipal Rose Garden. Continue straight ahead 2.8 mi. on gravel road. Turn right on gravel road 0.9 mi., then right again 0.8 mi. to monument on left side of road.

Here the highway follows the exact course of the Oregon Trail. In earlier days the graves of nine victims of the massacre were preserved. The present owner of the farm plowed them under, apparently more concerned with alfalfa-growing than with northwest history. Relocating them would be a good project for some civic group.

WHEN ALEXANDER WARD and his small wagon train reached the Boise River Valley they felt it was the climax of their trip. Behind were months of travel through the debilitating, never-ending desert heat. Not far ahead was a larger wagon train, giving them a confident feeling of security.

They drove off the road August 20, 1854, to rest and have lunch by the Boise River. The 20 emigrants, including Ward's wife, four sons and four daughters, John Frederick, Rudolph Shultz, Dr. Adams, Charles Adams, Samuel Mulligan, William Babcock and several others, were preparing to continue their westward trek when one of the Ward boys rushed up to cry that a horse had been stolen by Indians.

Several men were accompanying the party on horseback, and one of these, named Amond, was dispatched with three others to recapture the horse. The wagon train moved on toward the road, the women and children drowsing in the heat. Ward led the party on horseback, and the other men walked or rode by the wagons.

When they reached the road the emigrants were ambushed by a band of Snake Indians. Ward fell dead in the first flurry of shots. Amond joined the melee and was killed as he tried to rescue one of the Ward girls who was being dragged away. The rest of the men held off the hostiles until sundown, but the rain of arrows and rifle bullets felled them all. Although William and Newton Ward were shot through with arrows, they managed to crawl into the brush and hide.

Driving the wagons with the women and children into the bushes, the Indians tortured their victims, burning alive three of the Ward children.

The men in the larger wagon train ahead were quick to ride back when they heard the firing, but were too late. They buried the dead. Finding the wounded Newton Ward, they carried him to their train. William, unconscious, lay unnoticed in the bushes. He made his way to Fort Boise a few days later, the arrow still in his lung.

When three of the Indians were caught they were tried and found guilty. One was shot as he tried to escape. The others were hanged at the scene of their depredations. The gallows were there for many years as a warning to other warrior Indians.

56

THE AMBUSH: This part of the road follows the exact course of the Oregon Trail. The attack on the Ward party probably started here.

GRAVES PLOWED UNDER: The monument and park are dedicated to the Ward party. The gallows where the Indians were hanged over the graves of their victims were beyond the brow of the hill, slightly to the right and back of the monument.

THE PIONEERS
ON THE OREGON TRAIL

[15] Basing point: Caldwell, Idaho. The monument to the Oregon Trail ford is at the northwestern edge of Caldwell on U. S. Highway 30. It is on the left of the road as the turn is made to cross the bridge.

THE VAST new Oregon Territory was conquered by the ox team and the covered wagon; the farmer and his plow; the missionary and his grist- and sawmill. Never in all history has so great a land been won so quickly, nor by such peaceful means.

There is a tendency to make martyrs of the pioneers who joined the great movement on the Oregon Trail. They suffered many hardships, but it should be remembered that they were ordinary people seeking homes, health, wealth or high adventure. These motives, common to the peoples of all times, were what actuated their westward trek. Perhaps the very simplicity and naturalness of their desires made the conquest so complete, and won the West for the United States even against the carefully laid intrigues of the British.

Certainly the Trail tried the mettle of the men and their families. They never knew what tremendous obstacle or pathetic tragedy lay just over the next hill.

A. J. Splawn, who crossed the plains when only six years old, tells of childbirth, murder, and death from cholera on the Trail. He saw a scaffold on which was a rocking chair, the only available tombstone for a woman who had died bearing a child.

The Hays wagon train, described by Splawn, overtook a wagon with a sick child. Mrs. Hays contracted the disease while trying to help.

Cholera soon swept through all the younger members of her train. Three Hays boys died and were buried along the Trail. Soon Mrs. Hays, too, was dead. Her husband wrote "Naomi Hays" on the end-gate of a wagon and placed it over her grave. Then, because there was no time to stop, he moved along.

A few days later old friends of Mrs. Hays, the Yantises, passed the burial spot. Stopping their wagon they saw the gate with its brief memorial message. Mrs. Ann Yantis, mortally ill, said, "Take me to sleep beside Naomi." When she died two days later her name was written under her friend's on the wagon end-gate.

Such people, who risked all for a sick child, who wanted simply to be buried near a friend, or who could push steadily on after losing those close to them, built the West. They were not iron men. They were simply courageous, ambitious, and persevering.

58

OREGON TRAIL FORD: At the Boise River.

WILSON PRICE HUNT
AT FAREWELL BEND

[16] Basing Point: Ontario, Oregon. Go 29.6 mi. west on U. S. Highway 30 to Oregon highway sign on the right side of the road.

Viewing the rugged mountains to the north, with range on range, each higher than the preceding one, and the narrow canyon walls where the Snake cuts through, one can understand why Hunt decided to leave the "mad accursed river."

HUNGER, hardship and many good-bys were inevitable to those who settled the West.

The Astorian Overland Party left Missouri July 18, 1811. Wilson Price Hunt, personal representative of John Jacob Astor in the Pacific Fur Company, headed the group of 64 people and their pack train of horses laden with merchandise and supplies. Their mission was to meet the party coming in by sea at what is now Astoria.

Two months later, on September 26, they reached the Snake River, and on October 8 arrived at Fort Henry. At the fort they constructed 15 canoes, and left their horses in charge of Indians.

The swift Snake claimed a life at Caldron Linn, where a canoe upset. Discouraged, the party decided the river was unnavigable. An attempt to regain their horses was found hopeless.

The trip was reorganized. A group under an experienced hunter named Crooks started down the southern bank of the Snake. Hunt, with the balance of the party including Pierre Dorion and his Indian wife and two children, set out on the north bank.

When they reached what is now called Farewell Bend, where the Snake goes through the Blue Mountains, they knew they could not follow the river banks farther.

There, on either side of the river, the exhausted, cold and hungry parties camped. Hunt's men, so depleted that they were insensible to each other's needs, had to be forced to take food to the starving Crooks party across the river. One of Crooks' men, frantic at sight of food, overturned a canoe and was drowned. On December 22, 1811, the Hunt party, building a canoe out of hides from two horses they had acquired from Indians, sent some horsemeat across the dangerous river.

The Crooks party was at last ferried over the river. "Much ice had formed during the night," Washington Irving wrote in his *Astoria,* "and they were obliged to break it for some distance from each shore. At length they all got over in safety to the west side, and their spirits rose on having achieved this perilous passage."

Hunt and his party started for the mountains, with five horses carrying their remaining luggage. They finally reached Astoria.

Oregon Trailers, years later, called this spot Farewell Bend because they too were forced to leave the Snake and continue their journey overland to the Oregon country.

60

FAREWELL BEND: Here the Snake River enters Hell's Canyon, still almost a complete wilderness.

INDIAN COUNTRY: In Oregon Trail days the Indians ambushed several wagon trains here.

THE BIRTH OF THE DORION BABY IN THE WILDERNESS

[17] Basing point: North Powder, Oregon. To reach birthplace of the Dorion baby, continue 2.8 mi. west on U. S. Highway 30 to Oregon highway marker.

The country between Farewell Bend and the birthplace is arid. The highway today probably follows quite closely the route of the Wilson Price Hunt expedition. Even when it approaches water the road winds through a rocky canyon until it reaches the open Powder Valley.

ALTHOUGH called by the cryptic name The Woman, this mate of the guide to the Wilson Price Hunt expedition was by no means a nonentity.

Born in 1786, The Woman was a full-blooded Indian of the Iowa tribe. Her first name was unknown. She married or became the property of the half-breed guide, Pierre Dorion, at the age of 18. When the expedition started The Woman had two sons. Baptiste was five and Paul three.

During the trip down the Snake River, difficult even for an unhampered traveler, The Woman carried Paul on her back and led Baptiste by the hand. In frigid weather the party climbed the mountains and followed the ravines between Farewell Bend and Powder Valley. There was hunger to face and exhaustion.

Pierre Dorion, on the night of December 30, told Hunt that he and The Woman would be delayed. Suggesting the rest of the party continue the journey, he said he and his mate would soon catch up. There on the trail the third Dorion child was born. "Nature is easy in her operation in the wilderness," Washington Irving commented on this event in *Astoria*, "when free from the enfeebling refinements of luxury and the tamperings and appliance of Art."

Somehow Dorion had acquired a horse and saved it from the hungry mouths of his companions. After the birth The Woman was mounted on the horse, holding the baby in her arms. Paul lay in a blanket-cradle at her side, and Baptiste walked with his father.

Following the tracks of the expedition, Dorion and his family overtook the rest of the party the morning of December 31 in the Grande Ronde Valley.

MATERNITY WARD

This monument is just across the Boise River from Caldwell, Idaho. Madame Dorion helped in the exploration of both Idaho and Oregon.

OLD CHIEF JOSEPH
AND WALLOWA LAKE

[18] Basing point: La Grande, Oregon. Take State Highway 82 north 72.8 mi. to Joseph. From there go south on State Highway 82 to Wallowa Lake. Old Joseph's grave is on a knoll to the right of the road between the highway and the north end of the lake.

Old Joseph was first buried about 4 miles from the little town of Lostine. His body was later moved to its present location.

"I WONDER if everyone is up. It is morning, we are alive, so thanks be! Rise up." These words from his morning speech typify the life of Old Joseph. This splendidly built man, son of a Cayuse chief and a Nez Perce woman, had the determination and foresight necessary to make him a born leader of a great people.

Bred in the mountains, the Nez Perce Indians were tall, handsome, intelligent and peace-loving. Even among their red enemies they were usually willing to submit to a wrong rather than do a wrong. The tribe, led by Old Joseph, made its home in the Wallowa and Imnaha valleys.

In 1855 Governor Isaac Stevens and General Joel Palmer called a council of all the Columbia chiefs to buy their lands and confine the tribes to reservations. Although the records show an "X" following the name of Old Joseph, his son Young Joseph said, "My father . . . refused to have anything to do with the council because he wished to be a free man. He claimed that no man owned any part of the earth and a man could not sell what he did not own. Mr. Spalding (the missionary) took my father's arm and said, 'Come and sign the treaty.' My father pushed him away and said, 'Why do you ask me to sign away my country? It is your business to talk about spirit matters and not to talk to us about parting with our land.'"

It is thought Young Joseph confused the Treaty of 1855 with that of 1863, which Old Joseph did refuse to sign.

When Stevens urged him to sign, Old Joseph replied, "I will not sign your paper, you go where you please . . . I am no child. I can think for myself."

Old Joseph returned to Wallowa, "the land of the winding waters," after the council of 1863. Driving stakes around it he said, "Inside is the home of my people . . . Inside this boundary our people were born. It circles the graves of our fathers and we will never give up these graves to any man."

In 1877 the old chief, nearly blind, lay dying in his lodge. Calling Young Joseph to him he said, "My son, my spirit is going very soon to see the great spirit chief . . . You are the chief of these people. They look to you to guide them. A few more years and the white man will be all around you. This country holds your father's body. Never sell the bones of your father and mother."

"Then my father smiled and passed away to the spirit land," Young Chief Joseph later said. "I buried him in that beautiful valley of winding waters. I love that land more than all the rest of the world."

WITH THE GREAT SPIRIT CHIEF: Old Joseph's grave at Wallowa Lake.

WALLOWA LAKE: The beautiful land of winding waters.

THE BANNACK INDIAN WAR

[19] Basing point: La Grande, Oregon. Go 35 mi. west on U. S. Highway 30 to monument at Deadman's Pass in the Blue Mountains. The monument is on the right (north) side of the road.

The scenic Blue Mountains have much historic background. The hills are still scarred here and there with old wagon ruts of the Oregon Trail. In these mountains the Piutes, Bannacks and Umatillas made the last organized stand of the red man against white aggression in the Northwest.

Emigrant Springs, near Meacham, was a favorite camping ground of the Oregon Trailers.

THE BANNACK WAR, last organized conflict between Indians and whites in the Northwest, was highlighted by a dramatic personal encounter between a swift-riding chief and a straight-shooting colonel.

Bannack Chief Buffalo Horn, disgruntled by real or imagined slights suffered when he was a leader of the Bannack scouts under General Howard in the Nez Perce campaign, was ready for battle. His warriors, resenting the entrenchment of the whites in the West, willingly followed him. In particular, the Indians were irate because the settlers' hogs dug up and destroyed their traditional food, the camas root. Several pioneers were murdered on Camas Prairie. The braves raided Glenn's Ferry (see "Three Island Crossing"), commandeered the ferry and crossed the river, moving south.

In the first real battle at South Mountain near Silver City, Idaho, Buffalo Horn was killed. The disorganized Bannacks were then joined by the Piutes, a tribe from Nevada under the leadership of Chief Egan. They moved into Oregon, murdering and creating havoc as they went.

When white soldiers under Colonel R. F. Bernard overtook the tribes, a brisk battle began. Suddenly soldiers and warriors alike ceased fighting to watch a gripping spectacle. Chief Egan and Colonel Robbins of Bernard's command plunged into a personal duel. Spotting one another at the same moment, they rode toward each other, firing. The powerful Egan was admired by his tribesmen for his bravery. Robbins, an expert shot, also was known for his courage. As the reds and the whites watched the drama, Egan fired Indian fashion, leaning over his horse's side and shooting under its neck. Although he was well-protected, his firing was inaccurate. Riding erect, Robbins was grazed by bullets, but his aim was better. He sent one bullet through the chief's wrist, knocking him from his horse. As Egan tried to rise the colonel put another into his breast. Swooping onto the field, Indian comrades dragged their chief away.

Although the angry Indians made it hot for the troops, they missed their wounded chief. Lacking initiative to follow up their attack, they slackened fire. With nightfall the tribesmen vanished into the fastness of the Blue Mountains.

66

The mountains by now were thick with hostile Indians. Bannacks, Piutes, Snakes and Umatillas schemed and plotted to defeat their white enemies. On July 11, 1878, three men named Coggin, Foster and Bunker were attacked while journeying from the Grande Ronde Valley toward Pendleton. Although Bunker was wounded, Foster took him on his horse and the two escaped. Coggin fell wounded from his horse. The Indians piled dry grass on his chest, setting fire to it as the man lay dying.

Six companies of the 21st Infantry, two companies of the 4th Artillery and one troop of the 1st. Cavalry attacked the Indians near Deadman's Pass on July 13. The Indians again were forced to withdraw, leaving the bodies of five of their braves on the mountain battlefield.

Chief Umapine of the Umatillas and some of his warriors, deciding to join the winning side, offered to attack their erstwhile allies. Thinking the Umatillas were still friendly, the hostiles allowed them to approach. The treacherous Umapine and his men fired on their former comrades, the Piutes, killing Chief Egan.

The white soldiers were not quick to believe that Egan was dead. After his scalp was presented to the commander of the troops, that doubting man demanded further proof. Accordingly the chief's head and one arm were brought in to the white camp. Robbin's bullet hole in Chief Egan's wrist proved the point.

Although the pursuit of the Indians continued and a few more battles occurred, the Indian resistance was broken. Without their leaders, Buffalo Horn and Egan, they were hopelessly disrupted.

DEADMAN'S PASS: Traces of the Oregon Trail show in the foreground and through the trees at the left.

THE DALLES, FRONTIER TOWN OF THE EARLY DAYS

[20] Basing point: The Dalles, Oregon. From the southwest corner of Fifteenth and Garrison streets, turn south from the post office, up the hill to West Ninth Street. Turn right 5 blocks out West Ninth to Trevitt Street. Here turn left 7 blocks to the school. Then left 1 block on Fifteenth Street to the Historical Building. Signs are posted along the way.

The Historical Building is the only remaining building of Fort Dalles, originally called Fort Lee. It is said to have been the quarters of the medical officers.

From the Union Pacific Depot in The Dalles follow tracks east until at right angles with oil tank on Fort Rocks. Turn right across tracks past railroad workers' houses. Take path at back of Texaco office at end of railroad spur. The depression at the left is where Lewis and Clark took their observations. It is 752 paces from the railroad station.

The "high point of rocks" where Lewis and Clark camped has since been named the Fort Rocks. A handsome marker is being built on the highway some distance away, but the actual campsite is marked only by an ugly oil tank.

THE DALLES was an Indian gathering place long before it became a rip-roaring frontier town.

Here the narrows and rapids made a break between the navigable waters of the Columbia River, making it a natural campground.

In the fall of 1805 and the spring of 1806 Lewis and Clark stopped at The Dalles. "We formed our camp on top of a high point of rocks which forms a kind of fortification . . ." Clark wrote.

Daniel Lee and H. K. W. Perkins established a Methodist mission here in 1838, with little success. The Indians were not interested. After the Waiilatpu massacre the missionaries were not interested, either. The mission was closed.

Fort Lee, a vital post during the Indian Wars, was founded at The Dalles in 1849.

As Oregon Trailers flowed westward, The Dalles teemed with life and action. It was 1765 miles from the Missouri River. Eighteen miles a day was good time, by covered-wagon standards; thus the arrival at The Dalles meant the end of 97 days of laborious travel. From here on, the emigrants and their wagons traveled down the Columbia on rafts. It was a time for celebration.

As the years went by, more and more means of entertainment sprang up. Saloons rang with noise. Dance halls and gambling houses pulled in scores of celebrants. A. J. Splawn, in *Ka-Mi-Akin*, tells of a young gambler who started crying and wanting his money back when he lost at a gaming table. "A knock on the head with a heavy revolver closed the scene, and he was dragged to the door and thrown out into the street. Business went steadily on. It would take more than a human life to stop a game."

The Dalles was the most prominent outfitting point east of the Cascades, but its ever-changing stream of people soon made it a typical frontier town.

LEWIS AND CLARK SLEPT HERE: A view of the Columbia River east and north from Fort Rocks.

MEDICAL OFFICERS SLEPT HERE: All that remains of officers' row at Fort Lee (Fort Dalles).

MEMALOOSE ISLAND

[21] Basing point: The Dalles, Oregon. Go 14.7 mi. west on U. S. Highway 30 to Memaloose Point. The island, partly submerged by the waters of Bonneville Dam, can be viewed below and slightly to the east of the point.

Farmers along the river sometimes can be engaged to take a party to the island in a boat.

In the early days three pioneers were drinking at a saloon in The Dalles. They all agreed they wanted to be buried on Memaloose Island among the only honest men they knew. Of the three men—John Martin, Amos Underwood and Vic Trevitt—only Trevitt, who died in San Francisco, was buried there. His monument can be seen on the Oregon side of the island.

MEMALOOSE ISLAND was the island of the dead.

This ancient Indian burial ground was examined by Lewis and Clark in October, 1805.

Investigating the island, whose very name is the Indian word for dead, they found a building 60 feet long and 12 feet wide. Since both ends were open, they entered the great tomb.

". . . We observed a number of bodies wrapped carefully in leathern robes, arranged in rows on boards, and covered with a mat," their *Journal* reads. "This was the part destined for those recently deceased; while a little farther on there were bones half decayed and scattered about, and in the center of the building there was a large pile of them heaped promiscuously on each other.

"At the eastern extremity was a mat, on which were placed twenty-one skulls . . . the mode of interment being, first, to wrap the body in robes, and as it decays the bones are thrown into a heap and the skulls placed together. From the different boards and pieces of canoes which formed the vault, there were suspended . . . trinkets of various kinds, obviously intended as offerings of affection to deceased relatives."

Outside of the burial place they found piles of horses' bones. They assumed the animals were sacrificed to their masters at the funeral rites.

Why they buried their dead on the island was a question lost in the boundless time that passed as generation after generation of Indians followed the custom.

SHROUDS: Memaloose, the island of the dead, is slightly to the left of the center of the picture.

MISTY RIVER: Beacon Rock, the landmark that indicated to early boatmen the end of tidewater in the Columbia.

THE BATTLE
AT THE CASCADES

[22] Basing point: Hood River, Oregon. Continue 21 mi. west on U. S. Highway 30 to the Bridge of the Gods. Cross the Columbia River. Turn left (west) on U. S. Highway 830, 15.1 mi. to Fort Rains, a blockhouse on the right (north) side of the road.

There is an Indian legend concerning Beacon Rock, which is 4.4 miles farther along the same road. Wahatpolitan, an Indian woman, was about to be given to a chief she did not love. Scaling this rock with her baby in her arms, she leaped to her death from the peak. When the Chinook wind blows gently up the river, the Indians say Wahatpolitan's lamenting voice can be heard.

THE CASCADES were wide open for attack in 1856. These three small settlements were located on the gorge where the Columbia River cuts through the Cascade Mountains.

The river here was too hazardous for the steamboats to navigate with their cargoes of supplies. Great piles of provisions gathered, waiting to be conveyed overland. The Indians of the region, coveting these goods, chose a time when the Cascades were almost completely unprotected. The one blockhouse at the middle settlement was manned by only nine soldiers. The upper and lower Cascades had no defense.

Yakima Chief Kamiakin plotted to catch both of the upper river steamboats at the Cascades, kill the crews, burn the ships and massacre the settlers. He sent 30 of his Yakima braves on this mission. As they traveled they persuaded 20 Klickitats and the Cascade Indians to unite with them.

Kamiakin was to join them, possibly in an assault on Fort Vancouver which was weakened by the absence of all but one company. Colonel Wright had taken most of the companies into the Yakima country, while others had gone to Steilacoom.

The attack started March 26 early in the morning before the boats had steam. The crew of one boat started the fires, although three were wounded. One of the crew managed to back the steamer out into the river. A sharp toot of the boat whistle told the settlers he was off for help. The other steamer also got under way.

In the attack on the settlement, the Indians killed B. W. Brown, his wife and her brother. The remaining 40 settlers rushed to Bradford's store, a two-story log house. James Sinclair was killed when he looked out to see if more were coming.

The Indians threw burning torches on the roof which the men poked off with long sticks. Burning sections of the roof were chopped out or doused with brine from a pork barrel. A Spokane Indian boy, whom Sinclair had befriended, made many perilous trips to the river for water the second night of the siege.

The blockhouse also was attacked. The soldiers stationed there fought off the Indians with the howitzer, while the people in the neighborhood ran for the forts.

A friendly Indian warned the settlers at the lower landing, who clambered aboard two boats and started for Vancouver.

Only Lieutenant Phil Sheridan and 40 dragoons could be sent as relief from the depleted Fort Vancouver. More help came the morning of March 28, when Colonel Wright with 250 men returned on the two river steamboats. With the appearance of the troops many of the Indians fled.

Sheridan's plan to trap a group of the hostiles went awry when someone in Lieutenant Colonel E. J. Steptoe's command inadvertently warned the Indians by blowing his bugle.

Although the Yakimas escaped, the Cascade warriors were rounded up. They claimed complete innocence. Sheridan shoved his finger down the muzzles of their guns. They had been fired recently. Thirteen of the Indians were arrested, and tried by a military tribunal. Nine were found guilty and hanged.

A cruel consequence of this battle was discovered by Sheridan when he later searched for the missing family of a friendly chief. He found the mother, two boys, three girls and a baby all strangled to death, presumably murdered by a settler bent on vengeance.

THE MIDDLE BLOCKHOUSE: Now called Fort Rains.

DR. MC LOUGHLIN AND FORT VANCOUVER

[23] Basing point: Vancouver, Washington. Turn east on Fifth Street (U. S. Highway 830), going 4 blocks to gate. To reach Grant's house turn left 6 blocks, then right 0.3 mi. to the house.

This whole officers' row is old; many noted American soldiers, including Phil Sheridan, George B. McClellan and U. S. Grant, were stationed here.

To reach the site of the Hudson's Bay post, turn right through the lower gate. Follow road to the left, through the barracks, about 0.25 mi. to the site. Archeologists have excavated many ruins of the past here.

The oldest apple tree in the Pacific Northwest is to the left, behind the coal bunkers, near the fence on the lower road.

Fort Vancouver is a curious and motley collection of the old and the new. It has been a link in the chain of United States history since the founding of the Hudson's Bay post. In the Indian Wars, the Civil War, the Spanish-American War and the two World Wars, the fort has housed soldiers, each group of whom has left its mark.

IN THE critical years of rivalry between the United States and Great Britain for the possession of the Oregon country, Fort Vancouver was a bulwark of British domination.

The Hudson's Bay post was moved from Fort George at Astoria to Fort Vancouver in 1824 partly for political advantage, as the British hoped to hold the territory north of the Columbia.

Dr. John McLoughlin stepped into the ticklish situation of running the fort. Over six feet tall and of imposing manner, McLoughlin was the son of an Irish father and a Scotch mother. His long, pure-white hair earned him the name White Headed Eagle among the Indians. A firm but humane man, he demanded and received obedience from those under him. Indians as well as whites respected McLoughlin, knowing he kept his word.

A band of warlike Indians once appeared at the fort, giving the White Headed Eagle an opportunity to show his sense of humor as well as his knowledge of psychology. He sent a huge Highlander in kilts to meet the hostile group at the gate. Amazed, the Indians stared at the unusual sight. When another Scot paraded before them, playing a bagpipe, the tribesmen were thoroughly impressed. After gazing with complete awe, they left in peace.

Fort Vancouver was built inside a 750-foot by 500-foot palisade, 20 feet high. Within the timber fence were 40 wooden buildings and a stone powder magazine. Bastions stood at diagonal corners.

74

THE SANDS OF TIME

The ruins of Fort Vancouver were buried long ago. Now excavated, the remains of the bastion are pictured above, and the posts of the stockade at the right.

Although far from civilization, the fort's dining hall resounded through the years with ever-changing voices. The feudal-type bachelors' hall, resplendent with weapons and trophies, also whirled with social life. Marcus and Narcissa Whitman, John C. Fremont, Nathaniel Wyeth, Father Francois Blanchet, Jason Lee and many others enjoyed the gracious hospitality of McLoughlin and his wife. Mrs. Whitman called the fort "The New York of the Pacific Ocean."

In 1826 an English dinner guest at Vancouver, Captain Aemilius Simpson, remarked with amusement that a lady friend in London had given him some apple seeds to plant in the wilderness. As Simpson pulled them from his pocket Dr. McLoughlin accepted them in all seriousness. Apparently the whimsical wish of the Englishwoman appealed to him, for he later planted the seeds which sprouted into the Northwest's first apple trees.

A humming center of social activity, the fort also housed men of science. The Douglas fir was named after David Douglas, a botanist of the Royal Horticultural Society, who stayed at Fort Vancouver.

Dr. McLoughlin was completely impartial with his hospitality. Americans, British, Indians, all were welcome. His kindness lost him his job. After the treaty of 1846 ended British domination in the Oregon country, McLoughlin was removed from the post, being accused of friendship for the United States. His friendship consisted of helping the tired, often destitute, American emigrants. The White Headed Eagle replied to the accusations, "The Bible tells me 'If thine enemy hunger, feed him. If he be naked, clothe him.' These settlers were not even our enemies . . . If the directors find fault with me for this then they quarrel with heaven."

McLoughlin moved to Oregon City, where he attempted to take up a claim. Ironically, he was deprived of this privilege because he was an alien. Although he later became a citizen, it was too late to keep him from dying in poverty.

The United States Army established a post at Vancouver on May 15, 1849. Built to the north of McLoughlin's fort, on higher ground, it was first called Columbia Barracks. In 1853 it was renamed Fort Vancouver.

Although not actually on the Oregon Trail, the fort was the water terminus. Many settlers came down the Columbia, while some sailed around the Horn with Vancouver, Astoria or Portland as their objective.

Phil Sheridan and young Ulysses S. Grant were stationed here. Grant, who often spent his spare time changing scenery at the post theater, tried to augment his army pay by growing potatoes which were selling at $45.00 a sack. Although the soil in the river bottom was rich, his crop was ruined by the Columbia's June floods.

Throughout its history, under both British and American commands, Fort Vancouver has been a vivid cultural, military and social focus in the West.

FATHER OF THE MACHINE GUN

The Gatling gun, forerunner of modern fire power.

FOREIGN ANCESTRY

The apple seed that sprouted into this tree came from England over 110 years ago.

NO MORE PARADES: The parade ground and officers' row at Fort Vancouver still seem to ring with martial music and the tread of marching feet.

BACKGROUND OF A PRESIDENT: Young Lieutenant Ulysses S. Grant lived in this house before the Civil War. He built the little addition at the right.

LEWIS AND CLARK'S
WINTER CAMP, FORT CLATSOP

[24] Basing point: Astoria, Oregon. From city center go 6.5 mi. south and west on U. S. Highway 101 to junction with airport road. Take gravel road to left 0.6 mi. to where woodland road cuts off to the right up a hill. Leave car here and walk 105 paces up this road. The site of Fort Clatsop is in the little clearing at the left.

Souvenir hunters have really outdone themselves here. Not only have they stolen the bronze plaque from the monument, but they have torn down the surrounding fence.

IT WAS a drizzly winter, enlivened by some diverting encounters with Indian women, that Lewis and Clark's party spent at Fort Clatsop.

They examined the coast for some time before Captain Lewis reported he had found a spot where elk flourished that would be favorable for the winter camp. On December 7, 1805, the expedition settled near the mouth of the Clatsop River.

Day after day their journal mentions rain: "As if it were impossible to have 24 hours of pleasant weather, the sky last evening clouded and the rain continued through the day."

In spite of the continual drip of the rain from the dark evergreens, the party celebrated Christmas in their partially completed fort. "We were awakened at daylight by a salvo of guns . . . followed by a song as a compliment to us on the return of Christmas." The men who smoked were given tobacco; handkerchiefs were given to the others. Sacajawea gave Clark two dozen white weasel tails. With the rain sloshing down into the leaky hut, the group ate a Christmas dinner of spoiled elk meat, a few roots and some "mouldy pounded fish." Fleas added to their discomfort.

Late in December five men were sent to the ocean beach with large kettles to make salt. Filling Indian dugout canoes with water they allowed the brine to settle. When the water was poured off the top, that which remained was boiled until all moisture had evaporated. The salt was then scraped from where it was encrusted on the sides and bottom of the kettles.

Military discipline was enforced after the fort was completed on December 30. Indians were required to leave before sunset; the gates were closed and sentinels were posted.

On January 14 a whale came ashore. When a party set out to see it Sacajawea went along, pleading that it was hard to come so far and not see the ocean.

That there had been earlier white visitors was evident among the Indians. One woman had the name J. Bowman tattooed on her arm. Another, with freckles and red hair, could understand but not speak English.

Although an attempt was made by the Indians to murder one of the party for his valuables, ordinarily they were friendly. The Indian women sometimes were too friendly. Clark tells in the journal of one squaw who brought her seven daughters into camp, obviously intending to sell them to the men for a few trinkets. When a party of Chinook women encamped near the fort, Lewis and Clark exacted vows of celibacy from their men.

On March 23, believing the winter snows were melting in the mountains, the party started the long return trek. "At this place we have wintered . . . and have lived as well as we have any right to expect . . ." Clark remarked. "3 meals of some kind a day either pore elk meat or roots."

THE OLD SALT: The cairn at Seaside, Oregon, where Lewis and Clark's men made salt from the waters of the Pacific.

DREARY WINTER: The still rain-sodden site of Fort Clatsop, Lewis and Clark's winter camp on the Pacific Coast.

Dog meat tasted better with salt taken from this cairn.

THE JACKSON HOME
AND COURTHOUSE

[25] Basing point: Toledo, Washington. Go 7.9 mi. north of Toledo on U. S. Highway 99. The old building stands on the right (east) at Mary's Corner.

On the way you will see the St. Francis Mission about 2 mi. north of Toledo. Missionaries under Father Blanchet founded it in 1838. Once a vast timberland, this area still indicates its former wealth by huge Douglas fir and cedar stumps along the road.

HAD HE become a citizen earlier, John R. Jackson would have been the first American settler north of the Columbia River. Although he moved here in 1845, he retained his English citizenship until 1850, when he became a naturalized American.

Jackson was sheriff of all Oregon north and west of the Columbia River. He also held court in his home, as judge of Lewis County.

This home, built in 1847, was restful shelter for many an exhausted emigrant on the Oregon Trail. Governor Stevens and his family spent a night here in November, 1864, on their way to Olympia.

82

GRAY HOME IN THE WEST: The Jackson home and courthouse near Chehalis, Washington.

FORT HENNESS

[26] Basing point: Centralia, Washington. From Skookumchuck River bridge go 5.9 mi. north on U. S. Highway 99. Turn left on paved road 2.1 mi. Turn right on paved road 0.9 mi. to site of Fort Henness.

The Grand Mound cemetery across the road is a pioneer burying place. Recently the Masons have erected a monument dedicated to the Grand Mound Lodge, which surrendered its charter in 1868.

FORT BORST

Basing point: Centralia, Washington. From northern city limits, go 0.2 mi. north on U. S. Highway 99. Turn left about 3 blocks to Borst Park, on the right side of the road.

DURING THE Indian Wars of 1855–1856, the settlers, with justifiable anxiety, built a number of forts, some of which proved unnecessary.

Under the direction of Benjamin Henness, Captain of Volunteers during the Wars, pioneers constructed Fort Henness on Mound Prairie. It served as protection against threatened attack, although no actual onslaught occurred.

During the same period Joseph Borst, who had settled in the vicinity in 1846, erected a blockhouse on his farm. Raised to provide defense for his family and neigh bors, it was used only as a storehouse.

Nevertheless, there were enough outbreaks by the dissatisfied Indians to justify apprehension on the part of the pioneers. Governor Isaac Stevens was frequently criticized because many thought his one-sided treaties were responsible for the unrest that grew into the wars.

In a message to the Territorial Legislature, December 3, 1856, the Governor said, "I have had no end but my duty, no reward in view but my country's good. It is for you to judge how I have done my part, and for the Almighty ruler to allot each man his desert."

Governor Stevens was killed leading his troops at the Battle of Chantilly in the Civil War.

REFUGE

Above: The gate, now gone, of Fort Henness.
Below: The rebuilt Fort Borst.

THE SETTLEMENT
AT TUMWATER

[27] Basing point: Olympia, Washington. From state capitol buildings go south 1.9 mi. on U. S. Highway 99. Turn right at end of bridge. Go one block, then right again on old highway to the second bridge. Go past this bridge, not across, 0.4 mi. to Tumwater monument.

This was the real end of the Oregon Trail, as denoted by a monument at the old bridge.

Apt at graphic names, the Indians called this place Tumwater because of the peculiar drumming of the water in the falls. Old homes, rich in historical interest, can be seen a few blocks north past the monument.

TUMWATER, the first American town north of the Columbia, was founded by a Kentuckian with a stubborn streak.

Michael Troutman Simmons came to the Oregon Territory at the age of 30. In 1844 he wintered at Fort Vancouver, planning to settle in the Rogue River Valley. The British determination to keep Americans away from Puget Sound changed his plans. He resolved to go there.

That winter, with five companions, he started toward his goal but turned back at the Cowlitz River. In July he tried again, accompanied by David Crawford, George Waunch, Niniwon Everman, William Shaw, John Hunt, David Parker, Seyburn Thornton and Charles Eaton.

They selected a spot on the Deschutes River where it empties into Budd Inlet on Puget Sound. The settlement which they named New Market was later changed to Tumwater, a Chinook word meaning Throbbing Water.

Returning to Fort Vancouver for his family in October, Simmons interested others in making New Market their home. David Kindred, Gabriel Jones, George W. Bush, James McAllister and their families, and Samuel B. Crockett and Jesse Ferguson, bachelors, joined the settlement.

Harnessing the falls for water power, the men built a gristmill and, in 1847, a sawmill. Simmons sold the water power interests, in 1849, for $35,000.00. Buying a ship, he began a lumber trade with California. Cargoes of merchandise were brought back to be sold in the Simmons store in Smithfield. Smithfield, connected with Tumwater by a forest trail, was later to become Olympia.

PIONEERS' VISION: The dome of the state capitol at Olympia, Washington, as seen from Tumwater.

The monument at Tumwater.

INDIAN TREATY
AT MEDICINE CREEK

[28] Basing point: Olympia, Washington. Go north 8.2 mi. on Highway 99. Turn left on an unimproved gravel road 0.3 mi. to a clump of fir trees. On one of them is a plaque marking the place where the treaty was signed.

In the spring a blaze of scotch broom surrounds the traveler on this trip. The Nisqually Flats, where the treaty was signed, are a favored duck-hunting region in the fall.

THE FIRST treaty between Washington Territorial Governor Stevens and the Indians was at Medicine Creek.

Stevens, who was also Superintendent of Indian Affairs, negotiated a series of treaties, mostly unsuccessful, with the Indians during the years 1854 and 1855. Some of the tribes did not sign them. Of those who did sign, many were unsure of what they were signing, despite the presence of interpreters.

At Medicine Creek December 24 to 26, 1854, the Nisquallies, the Puyallups, the Squaxsons and others contracted a treaty with Stevens in which they relinquished title to all their lands, except certain areas which were to become reservations. In general, they agreed to keep peaceful and to free all their slaves. The Indians retained their fishing and hunting rights.

The government in return was to pay $32,500.00 for the land, plus $3,250.00 to be spent on preparing and equipping the reservations. In addition the United States would set up agricultural and industrial schools, supplying the teachers.

Edmond Meany's *History of the State of Washington* says, "It is altogether probable that the treaties contributed toward the causes of the wars that followed them." The treaties certainly tended to show the Indians that they were to lose their homes and to be forced to accept a foreign way of life.

FROM THE DIMNESS OF THE PAST: The treaty trees loom on the flats at Medicine Creek.

COUNCIL SMOKE: The prevailing haze of Nisqually Flats seems to come from old Indian campfires.

AMERICAN SETTLEMENT AT STEILACOOM

[29] Basing point: Tacoma, Washington. From southern city limits continue south on U. S. Highway 99 to the 8600 block. There Steilacoom Boulevard, a concrete road, cuts off on the right (west) of the Pacific Highway. Take this road 4 mi. to the Western State Hospital for the Insane, which is on the site of old Fort Steilacoom. Continue 2.4 mi. east on same road, to the town of Steilacoom.

Among the houses just inside and to the left of the hospital entrance are four that were used as officers' quarters in the old fort. One was occupied by General Phil Sheridan. All are in good condition.

STEILACOOM was a community of firsts.

Established in 1849 to protect the settlers against Indian forays, Fort Steilacoom was garrisoned by U. S. soldiers. Three members of the ship *Albion's* crew, William Elders, Frederick Rabjohn and William Bolton, settling in the environs, started the community of Steilacoom. In July of that year, Lafayette Balch, arriving in the brig *George Emory* with a load of goods, built a large frame store and trading house. In 1851 Balch built his home in Steilacoom of lumber that was shipped around the Horn from New England.

The first American ship to be built in this region was constructed here in 1852, founding Puget Sound's shipbuilding activity.

A faded brick building in the town was the first jail in Washington Territory.

The first Catholic Church north of the Columbia stood near the fort. When the fort was abandoned, the church was taken in three pieces into the town. Here, also, the first Protestant church north of the Columbia was erected.

Washington Territory needed help in caring for insane persons who were sometimes put ashore from visiting ships. During the years 1856–1869 the contract system was used in caring for them. On December 2, 1869, the Territory bought the buildings at Fort Steilacoom from the United States for use as an insane asylum.

SHADOWY FINGERS: The parade ground and officers' row at old Fort Steilacoom.

THREE-PIECE CHURCH: The old Catholic church at Steilacoom.

FORT NISQUALLY

[30] Basing point: Tacoma, Washington. The entrance to Point Defiance Park is at 45th and Pearl streets. Follow the signs on the drive through the park to Fort Nisqually.

What was left of old Fort Nisqually was moved to Tacoma in 1934 and rebuilt, using the old hand-forged hardware. Although not on its original site, Fort Nisqually is on historic ground. Here Indians, attacking from the sea, fought with a group of settlers in the early days.

THE SCENE of an Indian attack set off by an accidental gun shot, Fort Nisqually started as a 15-by-20-foot storehouse. In 1832 Archibald McDonald built the storehouse and left three men there. The following spring he returned, and wrote in his *Journal of Occurrences at Nisqually House:*

"May 30, 1833 Thursday. Arrived here from the Columbia with four men, four oxen and four horses after a journey of fourteen days, expecting to have found the schooner *Vancouver* here. She sailed the same day we started with trading goods, provisions, potatoes, seeds, etc., bound for Nisqually Bay, where we have now determined, should everything come up to expectation, to locate an establishment."

One of the men with McDonald was Dr. William Tolmie, who later was in charge of the post for Hudson's Bay Company.

The original Fort Nisqually was simply a wharf and a few small buildings on the water's edge. As the post developed, a stockade was built on the ridge above. In 1843 the fort was moved again to the position it occupied until abandoned.

Chief Patkanim of the Snoqualmies was responsible for an Indian outbreak in May, 1849. The first attack was on Fort Nisqually.

A band of warriors gathered near the fort. Patkanim was allowed to enter on his subterfuge that he had come to look for a Nisqually chief. During the conversation a gun was accidentally discharged in the fort. The Indians, mistaking this for Patkanim's signal to them, rushed the gate. Acting swiftly, the guards closed it before the Indians could storm into the fort. Two Americans, unable to reach the shelter before the gate shut, were attacked. One was killed and one wounded.

The settlers rapidly manned the swivel gun in the bastion. In the hubbub, Patkanim escaped. Seeing their onslaught to be futile, the Indians withdrew. Had the plot succeeded, the hostiles would have gained guns and ammunition for a sanguinary war on the settlers.

THE DIGNITY OF AGE

The only one of the original buildings moved from Fort Nisqually. The bastion, stockade and other buildings on the grounds in Point Defiance Park, Tacoma, although authentic, are replicas.

CHIEF LESCHI
OF THE NISQUALLIES

[31] Basing point: Tacoma, Washington. At Puyallup River Bridge on U. S. Highway 99, north from city center, turn right 0.7 mi. to cemetery. Walk up hill along old road 111 paces to Leschi's grave.

The buildings adjacent to the cemetery constitute the Tacoma Indian Sanatorium. It is a federal institution devoted to the care of the Indians of Alaska and the Pacific Northwest.

UNTIL embittered by the Medicine Creek Treaty, Leschi admired and often aided the white settlers in Washington Territory.

Son of a Yakima mother, this Nisqually chieftain was influential among both Indians and whites. In April, 1853, he assisted volunteers under E. J. Allen to build a military road to Fort Steilacoom, refusing pay for the use of his horses. About the same year a party of emigrants stalled at Naches Pass were saved by Leschi, who rushed without rest to bring them provisions.

At the Medicine Creek Treaty signing in 1854, Leschi turned enemy to the whites. The offer of bleak, useless land to the Nisquallies enraged him. He wanted good land where his people could learn to farm. Angrily tearing to bits a chieftain's certificate proffered by Governor Stevens, Leschi left the council. Although his signature was third on the list of chiefs who signed the treaty, it was probably forged.

Resentfully he told his tribesmen, "The pale faces . . . are going to send us to distant lands of midnight darkness, where we will never again see the light and where streams are too foul for even fish to live in."

He joined in various skirmishes against the army, culminating in the attack on the young city of Seattle in 1856. Although aided by Owhi and the Klickitat tribesmen, Leschi was repulsed. (See "The Battle of Seattle.")

As he was driven off he threatened to return.

When Governor Stevens offered a reward for his capture, Leschi went into hiding. At one time during his three years as a fugitive he volunteered to surrender to Colonel Casey at Fort Steilacoom. Because feeling was high, the colonel advised him to stay in the woods. Leschi's nephew, Sluggia, betrayed him for 50 blankets.

Leschi's trial excited a great deal of attention. Many white settlers and army officers joined in his defense, to no avail. He was declared guilty.

On February 19, 1858, Leschi stood at the foot of a scaffold looking up at the noose that was to end his life. With complete composure he climbed the ladder. "I felt . . . I was executing an innocent man," Charles Grainger, one of the executioners, said.

Leschi was first buried in the woods. When he was reinterred 35 years later many whites joined in the mile-long funeral procession.

". . . A LAND OF MIDNIGHT DARKNESS": A ghostly tree shadows the grave
of Chief Leschi.

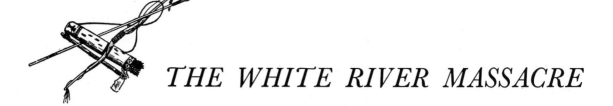

THE WHITE RIVER MASSACRE

[32] Basing point: Auburn, Washington. Take U. S. Highway 410 north 1.6 mi. to the monument on the right (east) side of the road. This is the monument to Lieutenant Slaughter. The monument to the victims of the White River Massacre is 0.1 mi. farther north on the same side of the road.

Auburn was first called Slaughter in honor of the lieutenant. When it became a railroad town, according to Edmond Meany, the citizens were embarrassed to hear the hotel guides calling, "This way to the Slaughter House!" They changed the name to Auburn.

Just north of Auburn is an interesting cemetery where Angeline, daughter of Chief Seattle, is buried.

King Street in Seattle is named after Johnnie King.

CHIEF NELSON of the Muckleshoot tribe, who often visited the home of Harvey H. Jones, was truculent when he called one morning. Leaving, he muttered that soon the "Bostons," as the Indians called the settlers, would own the whole country, and the Indians would be driven out.

Under the direction of Nelson, Indians attacked the Jones home on Sunday morning, October 28, 1855. They killed Harvey Jones, his wife, and Enos Cooper, a Jones' employee. Then they burned the cabin.

Johnnie King, a seven-year-old child by Mrs. Jones' former marriage, together with the two Jones children, a daughter of five and a son aged two, escaped into the woods. Hungry and anxious, they soon returned. Near the ruins of the house they found their dying mother, who warned Johnnie to flee immediately with the younger ones. Reluctantly he led the children toward a neighbor's house two miles away. The place was deserted. The three wandered, Johnnie carrying his whimpering half-brother much of the time. In later years Johnnie King described his desperation during the ordeal: ". . . I had nothing to give them or eat myself except bark and edible root . . . I was in danger from Indians and wild animals . . . An almost overwhelming sense of my danger and helplessness came over me as I thought of the coming night . . ." But before night came they met Indian Tom, a "friendly," who took them to Seattle. After spending some time on the U. S. Warship *Decatur* anchored in Seattle harbor, they were sent East to relatives.

At about the time of the assault on the Jones cabin, the Indians attacked the homesteads of William H. Brannon, George E. King and Joe Lake. They killed and mutilated William Brannon. Stabbing his wife in the heart, they dumped her body, baby in arms, into the well. George King and his wife were killed and cremated in the ashes of the home. Their children were kidnapped. The baby never was heard of again. Five-year-old George King was kept by an Indian who, devoted to him, wished to adopt him. George, however, was released to the whites the following spring. George King and Johnnie King were not related.

96

WATER ROAD TO SEATTLE

The White River down which Indian Tom brought Johnnie King and his baby brother and sister in his dugout canoe.

Joe Lake escaped to Seattle with a bullet hole in his coat.

William Brannon's brother, Joseph, attempted to avenge the massacre. Returning from a trip east of the mountains, he met an Indian wearing his brother's clothes. He killed him. It was said that in all he killed eight of the twelve Indians who were involved in murdering his brother.

The news of Joe Brannon's revenge became known, and for three years Chief Nelson remained in hiding. Brannon at last gave up his grisly pursuit at the request of his fiancee.

The contrite Nelson came out of hiding and lived peacefully near Auburn for many years. All of his children died of tuberculosis. Nelson believed this was punishment for his part in the massacre.

THE KILLING OF LT. SLAUGHTER

The grim events near Auburn on December 4, 1855, later were related by David Denny, a volunteer who was present. Roberta Frye Watt in *Four Wagons West* quotes him as saying:

"An Indian guide named Puyallup Tom accompanied Lieutenant Slaughter through the Green River country where he was to meet with the company of volunteers of which I was a member. It was cold and raining nearly all day. When near the spot where they camped they saw an Indian dog skulking along in the underbrush. Puyallup Tom said that the dog's master was not far off and to 'Closhe nanatch' (look out).

"Darkness came on before they reached the camp of the volunteers who were on the west side of the river. The Lieutenant found a small cabin in the opening in the woods and here he made camp for the night. They were all drenched to the skin so they stacked their arms and built large fires of fence rails around which the soldiers stood to dry. The Lieutenant did not put out any guards as he had not seen any Indians that day.

"He made his quarters in the cabin with his officers where they had a fire on the earth floor. As the night drew on the hooting of owls was heard. The guide told him that it was the Indians signaling to each other, but he said 'No, you're mistaken.' Puyallup Tom begged that the fire be extinguished, but the Lieutenant refused.

"He sent a courier to the camp of volunteers and three of their officers came to confer. The soldiers were around the bright fire and the Lieutenant was sitting in the cabin when the Indians fired a volley into their midst killing Lieutenant Slaughter instantly. The bullet came in between logs striking him in the heart. He made no sound save the sharp intaking of his breath and fell over dead.

"Two of the soldiers were killed and several wounded. The men crowded into the little cabin and Puyallup Tom ran out and kicked the fires apart.

"The Indians withdrew for a time. Finally two men who were in a fence corner heard them creeping back and fired on them."

98

THE BATTLE OF SEATTLE

[33] Basing point: Seattle, Washington. The monument is located on Third Ave. and Yesler Way in a little triangular park south of the County-City Building.

At the time of the attack on Seattle, thick forests where the County-City Building now stands afforded concealment for the assaulting Indians.

WHILE SOME Indians like Chief Sealth and his Duwamish tribe agreed fully to Governor Isaac Stevens' treaties of 1855, others still hoped to remain masters of the West.

Rumors of Indian uprisings began to circulate. Seattle settlers were frightened into building a blockhouse into which they flocked after the White River and Slaughter massacres at Auburn.

The sloop *Decatur* was anchored in Elliott Bay. Captain Guert Gansevoort of the *Decatur* sent a scout through the woods to Lake Washington on January 25, 1856. The scout reported that Klickitats and Yakimas from east of the mountains, under Chief Owhi, and Puget Sound Indians, led by Chief Leschi, were massing for an attack.

Indian Jim, a friendly tribesman, slipped into the blockhouse early on the morning of January 26 to warn the settlers that Indians were concealed in the woods. The warriors fired on the blockhouse and on the settlers who were running toward it. Their aim was poor. Doubtless they were unnerved by the grapeshot and "mox poohs" as the Indians called shrapnel, that the batteries of the *Decatur* were pouring into the woods where they were hiding. The fighting raged all day.

Robert Wilson, 15-year-old Milton Holgate and an estimated 15 to 20 Indians were killed.

In the evening the skies were red from the flaming homes of the Holgates, Hanfords and others that had been fired by the tribesmen. Shouting a threat to return, the braves moved on up the Duwamish, looting and burning as they went.

Although Indian troubles continued for some time, these hostiles never returned to make good their threats at Seattle.

PIONEERS'
LANDING AT ALKI

[34] Basing point: Seattle, Washington. From city center, go south to Spokane Street. Here turn right, going west to Harbor Avenue. Turn right and drive along Elliott Bay to Alki Point.

Here on the salt water beach, it is exciting to watch the ships heading oceanward. Sunsets are often magnificent from this point. There are picnic tables at Alki Beach and a warm-salt-water natatorium.

AT EIGHT in the morning of November 13, 1851, the little schooner *Exact,* commanded by Captain Isaiah Folger, anchored off a wooded point in Elliott Bay. As a group of Indians, including Chief Sealth, stared curiously from shore, 24 men, women, children and babies disembarked into rowboats to be carried to their new world.

As they rowed toward shore the wind whistled around them. The women looked anxiously through the rain at the primitive forest and watching Indians.

Although the Indians gave them no trouble when they landed, it was still wet, cold and cheerless. While the men carried supplies from the beach, the women stood weeping under the great dripping trees. The only shelter was a log hut with no roof. A passenger who remained on the *Exact* later remarked, ". . . the last glimpse I had of them was of the women standing under the trees with their wet bonnets all lopping down over their faces . . ."

Two optimistic settlers from New York State named the point New York. Another, more doubtful, added "Alki" the Chinook word for by-and-by. Although known as New York-Alki for some time, the name was eventually shortened to Alki. The city that grew up around it was named Seattle after Chief Sealth.

It is said that old Chief Sealth originally resented the town being named after him. The Indians believed that every time a dead man's name was spoken his spirit returned to earth. Sealth apparently did not relish this prospect for his future. Ultimately he was pleased with the honor of a city bearing his name. Certainly there is a well-beaten path between the spirit world and the earth if Sealth returns every time Seattle is mentioned.

BIRTHPLACE
OF SEATTLE

SEATTLE BY-AND-BY: The monument to the landing of the pioneers on the
beach at Alki.

CHIEF SEALTH

[34a] Basing point: Seattle, Wash. Take ferry at Colman Dock to Suquamish. Graveyard is Catholic cemetery on hill just back of town.

The site of Oleman House, the great longhouse of the Suquamish tribe, and the place where Chief Sealth lived until his death have been made into a state park. Continue along main road 0.5 mi. to where a sign on the left indicates a turn-off to the park. Take road (left) 0.3 mi. to park. This is a spot that, as Chief Sealth said, "thrills with the memories of stirring events." The only remains of the house which covered one and a quarter acres and had forty apartments is a row of snags at the water's edge.

"Today I met a rude, humble people . . ." Captain George Vancouver, exploring Puget Sound, wrote in his diary in May, 1792. Among those people was a child, Sealth son of Schweabe, chief of the Suquamish tribe.

Vancouver and his men were kind to the curious Indians. Perhaps that is why the lad who grew to be Chief Sealth, tall, broad-shouldered leader of the Suquamish and Duwamish tribes, never lost his friendship for the white man.

When Governor Stevens came to Seattle in 1854 to arrange the treaty with the Indians of that vicinity, according to Dr. Henry A. Smith, "old Chief Seattle's trumpet-toned voice" summoned the tribesmen to listen. After the governor talked, Chief Seattle (Sealth) replied with a speech which, as translated by Dr. Smith, has become a classic of the "rude, humble people." He said, in part:

"And when the last Red Man shall have perished, and the memory of my tribe shall have become a myth among the White Men, these shores will swarm with the invisible dead of my tribe, and when your children's children think themselves alone in the field, the store, the shop, upon the highway, or in the silence of the pathless woods, they will not be alone. In all the earth there is no place dedicated to solitude. At night when the streets of your cities and villages are silent and you think them deserted, they will throng with the returning hosts that once filled them and still love this beautiful land. The White Man will never be alone."

Sealth was thought to be about eighty years old when he died on June 7, 1866. Hundreds of pioneers and Indians came to his funeral services at Suquamish.

"DEAD, DID I SAY? There is no death, only a change of worlds." Sealth's own words would have been a fitting epitaph for his grave which looks out across the water towards Seattle, the city named after him.

OLEMAN HOUSE: The snags in the water were once supporting posts of the home where Chief Sealth and many important Suquamish Indian families lived.

THE BEHEADING
OF ISAAC N. EBEY

[35] Basing point: Coupeville, Washington. From Coupeville on Whidbey Island, go south on State Highway 1D 1.3 mi. to Prairie Center. Turn right on main side road 0.3 mi., then left 2 mi. to Ebey's Landing.

To reach Ebey's blockhouse and the Davis blockhouse from Prairie Center, take main side road right 0.3 mi., then turn left 0.4 mi. Turn right down lane 0.5 mi. Turn left on gravel road to cemetery, which can be seen on the hill. The Davis blockhouse is in the upper right corner of the cemetery. The Ebey blockhouse can be seen by receiving permission and directions at the farm of Frank Pratt Jr., at the end of the road. The blockhouse is about 0.25 mi. out in a field.

Whidbey Island is quite primitive, although it was one of the first areas to be settled in Washington. Deer are often seen in the heavily wooded hills and valleys and even along the road. Families of pheasant feel right at home in the middle of Coupeville.

The blockhouses were built during the Indian Wars of 1855–56 as protection against possible trouble. They were not used, as the Indian natives of the island remained peaceful.

PERIODICALLY, the Haida Indians paddled their trim 50-foot war canoes the several hundred miles from southern Alaska, via the Inland Passage, to Puget Sound. Coming as far south as Steilacoom, 50 or more to the canoe, they killed, burned, looted and took slaves as they traveled.

Handsome, powerfully built, and much larger than the Puget Sound Indians, they were fierce and warlike. At the same time their culture was the most advanced of all the tribes north of Mexico. Their huge sea-going canoes built of giant red cedar logs were marvels of craftsmanship. They apparently were the inventors of the totem pole. Certainly they developed the totem poles to fine examples of the sculptors' art.

Always a threat to peace, these northern tribes were dreaded by the settlers as well as by the Puget Sound Indians. Twenty-seven of them, including a chief, were killed in a battle with the men from the U. S. Navy ship at Port Gamble, October 20, 1856. (See "Haida Indian Battle at Port Gamble.") For a time it was thought this defeat would keep them out of Puget Sound waters.

But the Haidas sought revenge. They attacked, probably at night, the schooners *Blue Wing* and *Ellen Maria*. The crews were murdered and the ships either sailed away or sunk. No trace of ships or crews has ever been found. This helped to settle the score on the Port Gamble defeat. But remember, a chief was killed. The Haida code required the head of a white chief in payment.

They first selected Dr. J. C. Kellogg as the chief whose head they would have. He had a good boat and good clothes, to prove he was "Hyas Tyee": Big Chief. However, the doctor was not at home. The Haidas continued northward along the Whidbey Island coast. Seeing a man working in Colonel Isaac N. Ebey's hayfield, they stopped to

104

DEATH CAME BY SEA

Probably the ravine up which the Haidas crept to attack Ebey. His home was near where the farmhouse now stands. *Right:* The Ebey family plot in the old cemetery.

BLOCKHOUSE ON THE HILL: Built by Isaac N. Ebey's father, the blockhouse overlooks the site of the Ebey farm.

THE CHANGING TIDE: It may have been here that the Indians took to their canoes with Ebey's head.

ask if the owner of the place was a chief. Little thinking he was signing Ebey's death warrant, the man replied that Ebey was indeed a great chief.

The Indians camped on the beach. After dark, August 11, 1857, they approached the Ebey cabin. Calling the colonel to the door, they killed him and cut off his head.

The Ebey family, with guests they had at the time, fled through the woods to nearby cabins. Well-armed, the neighbor men hurried to the Ebey home. The Haidas, hearing them coming, rushed to their canoes on the beach, escaping in the fog. They took the colonel's head.

Two years later Captain Charles Dodd, of the Hudson's Bay Company, discovered the head of his friend, Colonel Ebey, in an Alaskan village. Risking his life to secure it, he returned the head to Washington for burial with the rest of the body. The Territorial Legislature gave Captain Dodd a vote of thanks, January 20, 1860.

DESTROYER: A dugout canoe of the type used by Puget Sound Indians.

SOCIAL SECURITY

Above: **The Alexander blockhouse in Coupeville.** *Right:* **The Davis block-house in the old cemetery on the hill.**

CHIEF PATKANIM,
HEAD-HUNTER

[36] Basing point: Marysville, Washington. Go 5 blocks north of the stop light in the center of Marysville. Turn left on Eighth Street. Go through the totem pole entrance to the Tulalip Indian Reservation. Continue on main road 5 miles to fork in road. Turn left 0.4 miles to the cemetery. Patkanim's grave is to the right of the gate toward the south side. It has one of the largest stones in the cemetery.

Notice the old council house, one of the best features of the reservation. Although it is deteriorating, it still has the odor of council fires.

PATKANIM, chief of the Snoqualmie and Snohomish tribes, was a contradictory character about whom many disputes have arisen. Some of this confusion originated from his having several brothers who were often mistaken for him. They were almost as puzzling as Patkanim.

He first appears in Washington history as a menace. He and his braves threatened Thomas M. Glasgow and A. B. Rabbeson when they landed on Whidbey Island, forcing them to return to Tumwater. Emboldened by this success, he led a party of Indians to Fort Nisqually. There the wily Patkanim gained entrance on the pretext that he wished to settle a difference with the Nisquallies. The soldiers at the fort, sensing trouble, called in the settlers and held Patkanim in the stockade. The prompt action averted a massacre although one white man was killed and one wounded. Patkanim escaped in the ensuing disorder.

Apparently Patkanim planned to kill the whites, then secure guns and ammunition from the fort. Thus well-equipped, he thought to drive the settlers from the Puget Sound area. One of his brothers, Quallawort, was hanged for his part in this affair. Patkanim was shipped to San Francisco.

There the versatile chief saw so many white men he decided to get on their side. Returning to Washington Territory he announced his everlasting friendship for the settlers. He became a trusted friend of Arthur Denny. At Mukilteo he signed the Stevens Treaty in behalf of his tribes. Governor Stevens distrusted him, as did the captain of the *Decatur*.

Patkanim warned Denny of impending Indian trouble in 1856. When the chief was seen lurking at the heels of a military party in the White River Valley, near the scene of Indian depredations, he was ordered arrested. Arthur Denny interceded for him, claiming that the Indian seen was Joe Kanim, and that Patkanim was on a hunting trip. Fortunately for Patkanim, he did show up with game that he had killed in the Cascades. It may have been killed during the time of the depredations, or may have been shot later. He was not arrested.

The military authorities offered a price of $20.00, during the Indian uprising, for the heads of hostile Indians. Patkanim had learned the value of money. He led his warriors in a ten-hour battle with chiefs Leschi and Owhi of the Klickitats and obtained several heads, which he sold. Fighting for the heads was hard and dangerous work. The ever resourceful Patkanim found it easier to kill his slaves, whom he valued very little, and sell their heads.

After he had made sufficient profit from this enterprise, he went to Olympia to collect his money. When he returned, an early settler recollects, "A fleet of twenty canoes was seen rounding Alki Point and approaching the *Decatur* in Seattle harbor, and as the occupants were decked in gala costume, with clean faces, we were at a loss to account for the unusual display until Patkanim came up over the gangway arrayed in citizen's garb, including congress gaiters, white kid gloves, a white shirt with standing collar reaching halfway to his ears, and the whole finished off with a flaming red neck tie."

Patkanim died in 1858. He was first buried at the mouth of the Snohomish River. When floods threatened to destroy his burial place, his body was moved to its present grave on the Tulalip Indian Reservation.

HEAD-HUNTER'S HEADSTONE: The grave of Chief Patkanim who sold the heads of his enemies to the whites.

HEADMEN'S HOUSE: The council house, now used as an Indian boy scout meeting-place, is still redolent of old council fires.

CONFEDERATE GENERAL GEORGE A. PICKETT AT BELLINGHAM

[37] Basing point: Bellingham, Washington. The old home is located at 910 Bancroft Street.

In 1791, just a few years after the American Revolution, the Spaniard Francisco Eliza sent a small ship here and named the bay Seno De Gaston. In 1792 British Captain George Vancouver sent Joseph Whidbey to chart the region. After hearing Whidbey's description of the bay, Vancouver named it Bellingham Bay for Sir William Bellingham of the British Navy.

CONFEDERATE GENERAL GEORGE A. PICKETT, leader of the famous charge at Gettysburg, also figured prominently in Washington's early history. He probably saved the San Juan Islands for the United States. As a captain in the regular U. S. Army, in 1859, his firmness and willingness "to resist all attempts at interference by the British authorities . . . by intimidation or force," in the face of three British ships standing offshore, was instrumental in settling a boundary dispute with Great Britain.

Pickett and his men built Fort Bellingham in 1856 to protect the settlers against the marauding Haida Indians from the north.

While in this vicinity, Captain Pickett fell in love with a Haida Indian girl. The Haidas were far superior physically and intellectually to the Puget Sound Indians. This girl was said to be beautiful by any standard. They were married, probably by the rites of the Haidas. The couple lived here happily until Mrs. Pickett's death shortly after the birth of their son, James Tilton Pickett.

When news of the Civil War came, Captain Pickett placed his four-year-old son in the care of a Mrs. Collins of Arcadia, Washington. The captain returned to Virginia, his native state, to join the colors of the Confederacy. He sent money for the support of his son and often wrote of plans to have him come East. However, Pickett, like the Confederacy, did not prosper. His son remained on the Pacific Coast and became a newspaper illustrator and painter of much ability.

PICKETT'S HOME: George A. Pickett and his Indian bride lived here.

THE PIG WAR
ON SAN JUAN ISLAND

[38] Basing point: Friday Harbor, on San Juan Island, Washington. Take main country road northwest of Friday Harbor 9.8 mi. to junction with a dirt road. Turn right here 0.5 mi. to British Marines' camp. The grounds overlook the British blockhouse which is on the bay.

To reach the American camp, continue 21 mi. on same road to the opposite end of the island, where there is a junction with a gravel road. Turn right on gravel road 5 miles.

"Who owns the San Juans?" was a question that occasioned various disputes between the British and Americans in the middle 19th century.

Charles J. Griffin, manager of the Hudson's Bay Company farm on San Juan Island, refused to pay taxes to Isaac N. Ebey, U. S. Collector of Customs. Griffin claimed the island belonged to the British colony of Vancouver Island. Thus arose disagreement between Governor Stevens of Washington Territory and Governor James Douglas of Vancouver Island over ownership of the San Juans.

The Fraser River gold rush had brought many Americans to the Northwest. A number of them, disappointed in their search for gold, sought good locations for farms. The San Juan American colony was composed largely of these men.

One of the frustrated gold seekers, Lyman A. Cutler, planted a potato patch in the good soil. A pig, owned by Charles Griffin, repeatedly raided the patch. Cutler, the American, protested to Griffin, the Englishman. The pig continued the forays. Finally, Cutler told Griffin, "Keep your damn pig out of my potatoes." To this Griffin replied, "Keep your potatoes out of my pig." The next time the pig plundered the potato patch, Cutler shot and killed it. Telling Griffin what he had done, Cutler offered compensation. Refusing the money, Griffin attempted to have Cutler arrested. Although a warrant was issued, it was never served, thanks to the "offensive defense" offered by Cutler and the other Americans.

This trouble showed General W. S. Harney, in charge of the army in Washington Territory, the necessity of protecting the interests of the Americans. He sent Captain George A. Pickett, with Company D of the 9th U. S. Infantry, consisting of 68 men, to the island.

The British warship *Satellite* arrived from Vancouver Island, July 27, 1859, on the same day that Pickett and his troops landed. July 30, Charles Griffin sent Pickett an order to leave the island immediately, claiming it was the property of the Hudson's Bay Company. Pickett replied he was there by order of his government and would stay until recalled.

114

"WAR OVER A PIG? TUT TUT!" The blockhouse occupied during the border dispute by British marines.

Two other British warships, the *Plumper* and the *Tribune,* arrived, bringing the British forces to 2,140 men and 167 guns. The British commander threatened to land his men and compel the Americans to leave. Pickett retorted that he would resist such a landing whether they disembarked "50 or 5,000 men."

The American troops were reinforced by Colonel Casey and about 400 men, on August 10. Governor Douglas and the Vancouver House of Assembly grew excited at the news of this additional landing of Americans. The speaker of the house complained, "More troops have been landed . . . We must defend ourselves, for the position we occupy today would make the iron statue of Wellington weep, and the strong statue of Nelson bend his brow."

About this time bluff, hearty Rear Admiral R. L. Baynes arrived. Baynes, Commander-in-Chief of British Naval Forces in the Pacific, supplied the necessary common sense to relieve the situation. He refused to go to war over the shooting of a pig. When told of Douglas' plan to drive out the Americans by force of arms, he shouted, "Tut, tut; no, no; the damned fools."

Finally a joint occupation plan was agreed upon. A detachment of Royal Marines set up the English Camp on the west shore of San Juan Island.

Thereafter, a few miles apart, the British and American soldiers lived in friendship, playing cards together and competing to show the greatest hospitality. Meanwhile the border question was being arbitrated by Kaiser William of Germany, at the request of the British and Americans.

On October 21, 1872, the dispute was settled in favor of America.

BOUNDARY MARKER: The monument at Point Roberts marking the extreme northwest boundary of the United States. Archibald Campbell, U.S. Commissioner of the Northwest Boundary Survey, had about reached a peaceful settlement of the dispute when hasty troop movements on the part of the U.S. and British military almost brought about a war.

# THE HAIDA INDIAN BATTLE AT PORT GAMBLE

[39] Basing point: Bremerton, Washington. Take State Highway 21 north 25 mi. to Port Gamble.

Port Gamble is the location of the oldest industry on Puget Sound still under the management of the families who founded it. Captain Talbot and A. J. Pope, both originally from Maine, came to Puget Sound on the ship *Julius Pringle* in 1853 looking for a good lumber-mill site. That of Port Gamble seemed suitable.

The exact location of the Indian battle is not known. There is a Clallam Indian village across the bay from the mill, but the Indians involved in the battle were Haidas.

DURING THE years of Indian trouble the settlers feared a war alliance between the Indians from the north and those of Puget Sound. The northern Thlinkits, Nootkas, Haidas and Tsimshians, swiftly paddling their large canoes, descended periodically on Puget Sound in raids for slaves and plunder.

The settlers appealed to Governor Stevens and Captain Swarthout, of the *Massachusetts*, a "fireboat," as the Indians called a steamer. Captain Swarthout found a large band of Haidas camped near Port Gamble. Attempting to persuade them to leave in amity, he offered to tow their canoes to Victoria. Accustomed to doing as they pleased, the Haidas refused to go. Swarthout's proposition seemed to them an indication of his fear or weakness.

He sent an officer ashore with a flag of truce to try again to persuade them to leave, on October 20, 1856. The Indians only taunted the officer. A howitzer was put ashore. After one more futile attempt to reason with the Haidas, Captain Swarthout ordered an attack. The Indians were driven into the forest, their canoes and provisions destroyed. Twenty-seven were believed killed by howitzer fire and the rifles of the landing party. The survivors, surrendering after two days of fighting, were taken to Victoria.

Although the battle of Port Gamble ended any possibility of the northern Indians joining forces with the Puget Sound tribes, the Haidas avenged themselves by further depredations, including the murder of Colonel Isaac Ebey.

POPE AND TALBOT'S GAMBLE

Whether or not the name came from the element of chance involved, certainly the gamble was a good one that still is rewarding the heirs of the founders of the mill. In this old photograph the Clallam Indian village is in the background across the bay. *Right:* This Port Gamble Church still stands.

CAPTAIN VANCOUVER AND DISCOVERY BAY

[40] Basing point: Port Townsend, Washington. Take State Highway 9, 15.1 mi. south to tip of Discovery Bay. The bay is in sight from the road most of the way. Or from ferry dock at Port Ludlow take State Highway 9E north 12 mi.

Discovery Bay was a hideout for early day smugglers bringing Chinese into the country. Tales are prevalent about sea captains who stowed the Chinese away in sacks so they could be dumped overboard handily if a government boat approached. During prohibition it was a rum-runners' rendezvous where hijacking was common.

CAPTAIN GEORGE VANCOUVER of the British Navy entered the Straits of Juan de Fuca April 29, 1792. Next day he passed Dungeness Spit. "From its great resemblance to Dungeness in the British Channel, I called a low sandy point of land New Dungeness," he wrote in his journal.

At about this time Lieutenant Baker of Vancouver's ship sighted a "lofty mountain" which Vancouver named Mt. Baker.

On May 2 Vancouver sailed his sloop *Discovery* and the armed tender *Chatham* into a bay which he called Discovery after his ship. The island at the end of the bay he named Protection Island.

He and his party explored these waters further while at anchor in the bay. According to his journal, "We found the surface of the sea almost covered with aquatic birds of various kinds . . . the Indians fished in the waters without paying any more attention to our cutter than if she had been one of their own canoes."

Vancouver left the bay for further exploration of Puget Sound May 7. He wrote, "As we advanced the country seemed to improve in beauty . . . and we saw a very remarkable high, round mountain." He called it Mt. Rainier, after Rear Admiral Rainier of the British Navy. May 13 he explored an inlet, naming it Hood Canal after the "Right Honorable Lord Hood."

During the next few weeks Vancouver discovered and named Whidbey Island, Bellingham Bay and nearly 70 other localities. Puget Sound honors one of his lieutenants, Peter Puget.

VANCOUVER'S DISCOVERY

Still beautifully scenic, it is little changed since Vancouver's ship *Discovery* anchored here. His men landed on the spit of sand shown in the center of the picture.

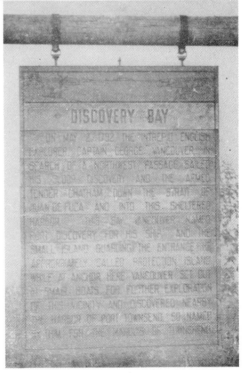

EARLY DISCOVERERS AND THE STRAITS OF JUAN DE FUCA

[41] Basing point: Port Angeles, Washington. The city of Port Angeles is on the Straits of Juan de Fuca. To reach Cape Flattery, the westernmost point in the United States, take U. S. Highway 101 west 42.2 mi. to Sappho. Here take State Highway 9A 33.7 mi. to Neah Bay. From Neah Bay a trail leads 5 mi. to Cape Flattery.

Tatoosh Island and Tatoosh lighthouse can be seen a half mile offshore. Neah Bay is on the Makah Indian Reservation. This was the location of a small fort built by the Spaniard Bodega y Quadra, and occupied by Spaniards for 5 months.

MICHAEL LOK, an Englishman, heard a story from Apostolos Valerianos in 1596. Valerianos was a Greek navigator who sailed for the Spanish under the name of Juan de Fuca.

Valerianos told Lok the Viceroy of Mexico sent him to the northwest American coast in 1592. "Hee followed the coast . . . untill hee came to the Latitude of fortie seven degrees," wrote Lok in 1625, "and that there finding that the Land trended North and Northeast with a broad Inlet of Sea between 47 and 48 degrees of Latitude: Hee entered thereinto, sayling therein more than twentie dayes . . . and found . . . very much broader sea than was at said entrance, and that hee passed by divers Ilands in that sayling."

Evidence to substantiate his story is the presence of the straits on maps long before they were discovered by Captain Charles Barkley, an Englishman, in 1787.

Shortly after Barkley's trip Captain John Meares, a retired British navy man, went a few miles in to the waters and named them the Straits of Juan de Fuca.

Meares was the first to import Chinese labor to America. Bringing Chinese men with Hawaiian wives to Nootka, he used them in building *North West America*, the first ship to be constructed on the Pacific Coast.

FARTHEST WEST: Cape Flattery, the extreme northwestern tip of the United States.

SEAGOING CANOES: Larger canoes of this type brought the warlike Haidas down from Alaska for their raids in Puget Sound.

SPANISH EXPLORERS AND DESTRUCTION ISLAND

[42] Basing point: Forks, Washington. Take U. S. Highway 101, 41 mi. south to Ocean Beach Park. On a turnout Destruction Island can be seen to advantage. It is about 4.5 mi. offshore.

Here you are traveling through the last frontier. The great stands of Douglas fir, the Pacific Ocean surf, the Olympic Mountains and the wild game so impressed Franklin Roosevelt that partly through his efforts the Olympic National Park was created.

SIR FRANCIS DRAKE perhaps was the first white man to visit the Washington coast. He sailed up the north Pacific coast in 1579 seeking the Northwest Passage which would afford him a short cut home to England, with plunder taken in raids against the Spanish. He claimed to have sailed as far north as 48 degrees before being forced by a storm to go south to refit his ship. Some authorities disputing Drake's claim say he sailed just past 42 degrees.

Apostolos Valerianos, known as Juan de Fuca, came as far north as 48 degrees. The great body of water wherein he "sayled" 20 days may have been the Straits of Juan de Fuca. (See "Early Discoveries and the Straits of Juan de Fuca.")

In 1774 Juan Perez, a Spanish sea explorer, sighted a high mountain which he named Santa Rosalia. Fourteen years later John Meares called the same peak Mt. Olympus. Perez discovered Nootka Sound, which he called San Lorenzo, and established Spanish claims.

On his ship *San Diego,* Bruno Heceta, accompanied by Juan Bodega y Quadra in the schooner *Sonora,* anchored in the lee of this island in 1775. Heceta sent 7 men ashore to the mouth of the Hoh River for drinking water. Indians attacked when they landed, killing them all and tearing their boat apart for its metal. Bodega y Quadra named the island offshore Isla de Dolores: Island of Sorrow.

In 1787 Captain Charles Barkley, in his ship, the *Imperial Eagle,* rediscovered the Straits of Juan de Fuca. He sent a landing party of six men ashore at the mouth of the Hoh. They also were killed by Indians. Barkley called the stream Destruction River.

The island offshore, Isla de Dolores, has since been named Destruction Island and the original Indian name of Hoh restored to the river.

Captain Barkley was accompanied by his wife, who was probably the first white woman to see the Washington coastline.

1 24

FLEEING BEFORE THE STORM: The trees all along the Washington coast-line turn their backs to the winds.

DESTRUCTION ISLAND: Five miles offshore.

CHIEF JOSEPH'S DEATH AT NESPELEM

[43] Basing point: Coulee City, Washington. From Coulee City on U. S. Highway 10A take Highway 2F north 28 mi. to Grand Coulee. Cross bridge just below the dam and proceed north 15 miles to Nespelem. At the extreme north end of town, on a little hill, is a Catholic cemetery. Chief Joseph's grave faces the gate in the southeast corner.

The grave of Yellow Wolf is near that of Chief Joseph. Some historians contend that old Chief Kamiakin is also buried here. However, another Kamiakin, grandson of the chief, told the authors that the old chief was buried secretly at Sprague in a hidden grave. Nespelem is the headquarters of the Colville Indian Reservation. Many of the Indians living here are descendants of the fierce Yakimas.

To the Indians he was Hin-Mah-Too-Yah-Lat-Kekt, Thunder Rolling in the Mountains. To others he was the brilliant young Chief Joseph, feared for his clever war strategy, and admired for his intellect, his profound spirituality and his rare gift of speech.

"Whenever the white man treats the Indian as they treat each other," Joseph once said, "then we shall have no more wars. We shall be all alike—brothers of one father and one mother, with one sky above us and one country around us and one government for all. Then the Great Spirit Chief . . . will smile on this land and send rain to wash out the bloody spots made by my brothers' hands upon the face of the earth . . . I hope that no more groans of wounded men and women will ever go to the ear of the Great Spirit Chief above, and that all people may be one people."

Of his surrender at Bear Paw, Chief Joseph said, "General Miles had promised that we might return to our country with what stock we had left." The pledge was an empty one: the captives were sent to Fort Leavenworth as prisoners.

Accustomed to high, pine-scented mountain air, the Indians suffered terribly here and many died. "The Great Spirit Chief who rules above seemed to be looking the other way," Chief Joseph said of this period, "and did not see what was being done to my people."

For eight years the Nez Perce were shunted from one reservation to another. At the end of that time, all that remained of those General Miles had captured were sent West. One hundred eighteen were returned to Lapwai, but high feeling made it unsafe to take Joseph to Idaho. He and 150 of his tribesmen were taken to Nespelem, on the Colville Indian Reservation.

Although he lived at Nespelem in comparative comfort, Joseph always yearned for his boyhood home at Wallowa. Sitting before his fire, September 21, 1904, Hin-Mah-Too-Yah-Lat-Kekt fell forward silently in death. The wish he had once made was granted him. "Let me be a free man, free to travel, free to stop, free to work, free to trade where I choose, free to choose my own brothers, free to follow the religion of my fathers, free to think and talk and act for myself."

**THUNDER ROLLING
OVER THE MOUN-
TAINS**

A storm brews over
Grand Coulee and Nes-
pelem.

**"HEAR ME MY
CHIEFS"**

The pointed stakes in
back of Chief Joseph's
grave were used at the
time of burial to dis-
play prized possessions
of the deceased Indians.

FORT COLVILE
AND FORT COLVILLE

[44] Basing point: Spokane, Washington. Take U. S. Highway 395 north 91 mi. to Kettle Falls. On State Highway 22, go north 6.1 mi. to junction with gravel road. Turn left 0.5 mi. to the site of old Fort Colvile.

Old Fort Colvile, built by Hudson's Bay men, is not to be confused with the American Fort Colville, at first known as Harney's Depot, located about 3 miles from the town of Colville.

FURS AND GOLD played leading roles in the drama of Fort Colvile.

Constructed in 1826, it was named after Andrew Colvile, Governor of the Hudson's Bay Company. The fur trade in the northern part of Washington Territory centered here. The discovery of gold near Colvile made the fort the outfitting point for gold seekers in the region.

Governor Isaac Stevens and Captain George B. McClellan were welcomed at the fort in 1853 by the factor, Angus MacDonald. He had a plentiful supply of liquor, and wrote, ". . . The Governor was rather fond of it. 'Mac,' he said, 'this is powerful wine.' The Captain put his arm around my neck and whispered in my ear, 'Mac, my proud father, too, was at Culloden,' . . . and slipped from the sofa to the floor."

Harney's Depot was built in the summer of 1859 and occupied by Major Pinkney Louganbeel and four companies of the 9th U. S. Infantry. Its name was later changed to Fort Colville, with an extra "l" added.

The gold rush made a brawling, fighting frontier town of Colville. Roaming outlaws of the West were attracted there by the easy money. In 1861, soldiers raided the Chinese laundry and pilfered all the clothing. The next year a lieutenant from the fort murdered a man. No one dared testify against him so he went free.

The over-abundance of liquor seemed to enhance lawlessness. Finally Major Curtis, commanding officer at the fort, broke up the town's distillery and confiscated the whiskey. This somewhat subdued Colville.

HERE STOOD
FORT COLVILLE
OF THE
HUDSON'S BAY
COMPANY
1826 — 1871
GEORGE SIMPSON
JOHN WORK
ARCHIBALD McDONALD
ANGUS MacDONALD

ERECTED BY THE
WASHINGTON STATE
HISTORICAL SOCIETY
1938

HERE BEGAN TRADE
FARMING MILLING
AND STOCK RAISING
IN STEVENS COUNTY

THE BATTLE OF FOUR LAKES

[45] Basing point: Spokane, Washington. From overpass on U. S. Highway 10 just before leaving Spokane city limits, continue west 7.2 miles. Here at junction take U. S. Highway 395 south 7.5 mi. to Four Lakes monument. Take gravel road to the right. This road goes past the Four Lakes.

This is a natural battlefield. Large rocks for protection, timber patches for cover, and hilltops from which to scout the approaching enemy, make it a fit setting for the tragic tableau of war.

AFTER THE Steptoe defeat, it was decided at a council in Fort Vancouver that the Indians must be thoroughly chastened. Colonel Wright led 700 well-equipped and trained men to inflict this punishment.

The first detachment left Fort Walla Walla August 7, 1858. The soldiers, well into the Spokane country by August 30 and 31, observed Indians on the hilltop. These Indians were placed to lead the soldiers toward the main force of hostiles. Carefully, they had chosen their battleground on two high hills near the four lakes: Silver, Meadow, Clear and Granite. The tribesmen were very sure of themselves after their Steptoe success.

They fired the grass, and under cover of the smoke, charged Wright's supply train but were driven off.

In the morning the troops found the warriors had occupied the hills. A pine forest at the right swarmed with them. Several hundred braves were riding furiously back and forth on the open plain.

This time the troops, with their improved equipment, outmatched their foe. First the cavalry attacked, then the infantry. The Indians used their old tactics of riding up, firing, then dashing away. They were met with Minnie balls from Wright's artillery. Deserting their position on the hills, the warriors were driven out of the woods onto the plain. The cavalry charged among them, cutting down with sabers all within reach.

The fight lasted four hours. There were no casualties among the troops. It is believed the Indian losses were heavy. These losses could never be estimated accurately, because of the Indian practice of carrying away their dead.

HILLTOP TO HILLTOP

The Indians learned the value of a position on a hill from Steptoe and his men, but even with this advantage they were unable to stand against the superior weapons of Wright's army in the Battle of Four Lakes.

BATTLE OF SPOKANE PLAINS

[46] Basing point: Spokane, Washington. Take Highway 10 west 7.2 mi. to junction with U. S. Highway 395. Continue on Highway 10A 4.3 mi. to monument on the left (north) side of the road.

HORSE SLAUGHTER CAMP

Basing point: Spokane, Washington. Take Highway 10 east from Spokane 17.6 mi. to monument on left (north) side of road.

COLONEL WRIGHT gave his men and horses a rest following the Battle of Four Lakes. The march was resumed September 5, 1858.

On reaching a prairie the troops detected Indians at the edge of a timbered area about three miles away. The braves set fire to the grass. Realizing the danger of an assault under cover of a smoke screen, Wright ordered his men to attack.

Howitzer fire drove the Indians from the woods. Dislodged from their next positions by Wright's infantry, they were harried by the cavalry as they fled. A band of Indians, forced from the top of one table rock, gained another only to lose it also. When a large party of hostiles gathered, Wright used the artillery.

That day the troops fought Indians for 14 miles of their 25-mile march. One soldier was wounded.

The soldiers made camp on the Spokane River, at the present site of Fort George Wright, the night of September 5. After one day of rest, they moved about two miles above the falls, on September 7.

One of the Indian leaders, Garry, came to the camp expressing his desire to cease fighting. He was sent back with a demand for unconditional surrender. Next morning Spokane Chief Pohlatkin and nine braves entered the camp. One of them was a murder suspect who was tried, found guilty and executed.

The Indians, preparing a general retreat, started to drive their stock to the south on September 8. The dragoons intervened and the cavalry drove the herders away, near Liberty Lake. The 800 horses the soldiers captured were at first corralled next to Colonel Wright's camp on the Spokane River. Fearing the Indians might stampede the horses to regain them, perhaps taking some of the cavalry horses also, Wright ordered the animals killed. Two companies of troops were detailed for this grisly duty. It was nearly two days before the pogrom was completed. Long afterward the site was marked with piles of bones. It became known as Horse Slaughter Camp.

The Indians, who had planned to recapture their horses without much trouble, knew the war was over when the animals were slaughtered. They surrendered at the Coeur d'Alene Mission a few days later.

ROCK MONUMENT ON A ROCKY BATTLEFIELD
The monument to the Battle of Spokane Plains.

HORSE ABATTOIR

STEPTOE'S DEFEAT
IN THE PALOUSE HILLS

[47] Basing point: Spokane, Washington. From Spokane, take U. S. Highway 195 south 34.7 mi. to Rosalia. The monument can be seen about 0.25 mi. east of Rosalia on top of the hill overlooking the town. It can be reached by taking the cemetery road which runs directly to the monument.

Endless wheatfields cover the rolling hills in the vicinity of Rosalia. It is the famed Palouse country about which Zane Grey wrote in *Desert of Wheat*.

INDIAN UNREST became general during the spring of 1858. In the Walla Walla Valley a band of Palouse drove off a herd of livestock, some of which belonged to the army. Two prospectors were killed on their way to Colville. Alarmed settlers requested protection.

Lieutenant Colonel Edward J. Steptoe was in command of the Regulars at Fort Walla Walla near Steptoe City, now called Walla Walla. On May 6 he set out with three companies of dragoons and part of a company of infantry, totaling 152 men and six officers, to investigate conditions at Colville. He also planned to round up the thieves who had stolen the livestock, if possible.

It was a badly equipped party. Aside from two mounted howitzers, the armament was a miscellany of either outmoded or difficult weapons. The short muskets some carried had an extremely limited range. Others had rifles with a better range, but which could not be loaded on horseback. Most of the men had muzzle-loading pistols, although a few had revolvers. The cavalry had no sabers. To further add to their danger, the chief packer, who did not have room for all of his supplies, left behind part of the ammunition!

On May 16 Steptoe's column encountered about 600 Coeur d'Alene, Palouse and Spokane Indians. They wanted no soldiers in their territory and voiced their intention to fight to prevent them from coming. Seeing a battle inevitable if he continued, Steptoe began a retreat toward Walla Walla the morning of May 17.

The combat began as the column crossed a stream, to start with at very long range. Soon the Indians discovered the fire from the antiquated weapons of the troops was ineffective. They rode in closer. The dragoons were ordered to conserve their ammunition because of the shortage. A running fight developed, with the troops maneuvering to keep out of the gullies and attempting to find favorable positions on the ridges and hilltops.

As the retreat continued Lieutenant William Gaston was killed. Encouraged by the death of an officer, the Indians massed and charged his company. Fighting was equally heavy with the other companies. Captain Oliver Taylor was fatally wounded. A hand-to-hand conflict developed over his body, the dragoons using clubbed rifles

134

TREES FOR REMEM-
BRANCE

Right: The hilltop where Steptoe's exhausted men fought through an afternoon and part of a night.

Lower: The grove of trees planted on the battlefield in memory of the engagement.

instead of the sabers they so sorely lacked. The dragoons succeeded in recovering his body and carried it within their lines.

Steptoe realized that his men, pressed as they were, could not continue to move much longer. He chose the spot where the monument now stands as a place that might be defended as long as the ammunition held out. The column moved up to the ridge. At its crest, where the ground fell away sharply to the creek below, the men dismounted. Entrenching themselves as best they could in a circle, they lay flat on their bellies in the tall grass. Surrounding the hill the Indians attempted to creep up, with grass tied in their hair as camouflage. They were driven off twice, but by nightfall the soldiers had only about three rounds of ammunition left per man. The men were sure that when daylight came death would come with it.

In desperation, Steptoe and his officers decided to attempt a rush through the night to the Snake River. The dead were buried. The howitzers were dismantled, the carriages being hidden in the creek and the gun barrels buried on the top of the hill. The wounded were lashed to their horses. Light colored horses were blanketed so they could not be seen so easily. Every possible precaution was taken.

Many of the exhausted men had fallen asleep. Silently they were searched out in the tall grass. When all were aroused, the column moved off quietly through an unguarded pass between the Indian campfires. Safely through the Indian lines they broke into a gallop, heading for the Snake River which was reached about 10 o'clock the following night. There the troops camped in the security of a friendly Nez Perce village. The next day they started for Fort Walla Walla which they reached without further mishap.

Six men were killed and 11 wounded in this battle. Two were so critically injured they could not complete the trip to the Snake. Left by the trail, one died and the other was killed by the pursuing Indians. The bodies of the men were later brought to Walla Walla and buried with military honors. The two officers were buried in the cadet's cemetery at West Point.

THE EYES OF THE INDIANS

Scouts were stationed on high points like this to watch the movements of Steptoe's columns—an effective substitute for the airplane reconnaissance of modern warfare.

DEPARTMENT OF HIGHWAYS

"STEPTOE BUTTE"

THE SOLITARY PEAK TO THE NORTH IS STEPTOE BUTTE, OVERLOOKING THE SCENE OF THE BATTLE OF STEPTOE BUTTE WHERE, ON MAY 17, 1858, A BODY OF DRAGOONS UNDER THE COMMAND OF COLONEL E. J. STEPTOE, WHILE PROCEEDING FROM WALLA WALLA TO SPOKANE WAS ASSAILED BY A FORCE OF SPOKANE, PALOUSE AND COEUR D'ALENE INDIANS BADLY DEFEATED AND DRIVEN BACK IN PRECIPITATE RETREAT TO THE SNAKE RIVER HOTLY PURSUED BY THE TRIUMPHANT INDIANS. THERE THE DRAGOONS WERE SAVED FROM MASSACRE BY THE FRIENDLY NEZ PERCE WHO FERRIED THEM SAFELY IN CANOES AND BOLDLY INTERPOSED BETWEEN THEM AND THE PURSUING INDIANS

THE MULLAN ROAD

[48] Basing point: Coeur d'Alene, Idaho. Take Highway 10 east 27.6 mi. A white monument to Mullan stands on the left (north) side of the road. Take the trail, a few feet west of the monument, about 50 paces to the Fourth of July Tree.

In this region the road goes through one of the world's finest stands of virgin white pine.

HACKING OUT 624 miles of road in the 19th century was a tremendous and perilous undertaking. The Mullan Road, built for military purposes, was one of the most noted of the early wagon trails.

It extended from Fort Benton, where navigation on the Missouri River ceased, to Walla Walla. About 100 men under Lieutenant John Mullan started construction at Walla Walla in 1858.

Indians interfered, but the men resumed work on the project in 1859. Until 1863 they labored over prairie lands, through almost impenetrable forests, over the rugged Bitterroot Mountains, and across the open-timbered tablelands. It was not much of a road; Father Cataldo remarked that ". . . Mullan just made enough of a trail so he could get back."

But those early roads were formed more by the trample of many feet and the roll of many wagons than they were by construction crews. The Mullan Road at once felt the trample and the roll, for it was a path to the gold fields as well as to the Oregon country.

On July 4, 1861, Mullan and his road-builders camped in a canyon near the present Coeur d'Alene. One of the men carved the date and his initials on a pine tree, and the gorge now bears the name "Fourth of July Canyon."

MONUMENT TO A ROAD
BUILDER

NO FOOL'S NAME NOR FOOL'S FACE

The man who carved his initials on this tree in
Fourth of July Canyon changed a lonely place into
a public park.

THE SACRED HEART MISSION AT CATALDO

[49] Basing point: Coeur d'Alene, Idaho. Go 36 mi. east on U. S. Highway 10. Here take gravel road on right, marked by sign "Cataldo Mission," 0.25 mi. to the mission. It can be seen on a hill to the right as you approach the 36 mi. mark on Highway 10.

This is the edge of the Coeur d'Alene mining district, one of the world's richest deposits of lead, silver and zinc. The Coeur d'Alene section has created fortunes and taken lives. Late in the 19th century the Bunker Hill and Sullivan mine was the scene of bloody industrial strife, culminating in the assassination of Idaho's Governor Steunenberg.

Back of the mission's altar, handprints of the Indian workmen still show in the mud-packed wall.

BUILDING A MISSION in 1848 took resourcefulness and many industrious hands. The Sacred Heart Mission at Cataldo, established by Father DeSmet in the fall of that year, was built by Indians out of whatever material was at hand.

Under the actual supervision of Father Ravalli they constructed the mission of logs nailed with wooden pegs. Willows were used to tie the beams together. They wove twisted strands of wild grass through the beams and packed mud from the river in the chinks. Father Ravalli hand carved the wooden altar statues and painted them with Indian dyes.

The building was opened for services in 1852 or '53, although it was under construction for 20 years and not completed until 1868.

When the boundaries of the Coeur d'Alene Indian Reservation were changed, in 1877, the mission was abandoned.

PEACE: The Sacred Heart Mission at Cataldo.

"LISTEN TO THE BLACKROBES . . ." The interior of the church at Sacred Heart Mission. The figures on each side of the altar were hand carved of wood by Father Ravalli.

HELLGATE

[50] Basing point: Missoula, Montana. From the post office take U. S. Highway 10, 1.8 mi. to city limits. About 50 yards west of this point, turn left on paved road along the river. Go 3.2 mi. on this road to a board marker on left side of road. Take lane to the left 0.1 mi. to farmhouse. The buildings here are all that is left of Hellgate.

To reach the White House, continue on main road 0.25 mi. from board marker to another country lane on the left. Go down this road about 0.3 mi. to its end at the mission.

Spry Will Cave, a Missoulan who was the first white child born at Alder Gulch, has graphic memories of frontier life. Concerning Hellgate, he commented that these old tumble-down buildings saw much of the rugged, picaresque early western life. At least one man was murdered here. Boldt's Saloon was famed far and wide among miners and trappers. Higgins and Worden's was the first store in western Montana. Vigilantes hung road agents from the corral fence.

Will Cave took us to St. Michael's Mission where a pretty young woman answered the door. When he asked the location of the old mission cemetery, she replied she knew nothing about either cemetery or mission. She was quite astonished when told she was living in one of Montana's oldest churches.

ALTHOUGH INDIAN activities gave Hellgate its name, white men helped make the name appropriate.

Fierce, frequent attacks by Blackfeet upon the Salish and Flathead tribes at the mouth of this canyon caused the French Canadians to call it Porte de l'Enfer, or Gate of Hell. A natural, traditional thoroughfare for the Nez Perce, Salish and other tribes on their way to buffalo country, the narrow canyon walls and heavily wooded hills made the territory particularly adaptable to the ambush tactics of the Blackfeet.

Lewis and Clark camped at the confluence of Rattlesnake Creek and Clark's Fork. The Mullan Military Road went through Hellgate Canyon.

Trading posts and a few cabins grew up at Hellgate, with the usual result. Frontiersmen were not all good men. Tiny Hellgate had its share of brigands drifting in and out.

On a frigid January night in 1864, vigilantes from Alder Gulch rode into the little settlement. They were after Cyrus Skinner's road agents who, they heard, had been frequenting Higgins and Worden's store. Rounding up six of the desperadoes, the vigilantes tried them, found them all guilty and sentenced them to be hanged.

One of these, George Shears, willingly climbed a ladder in the barn at the Van Dorn ranch where he was to be executed. With the noose around his neck and the rope thrown over a beam, he looked down on the men who had judged him. "Gentlemen," he inquired, "I am not used to this business, never having been hung before. Shall I jump off or slide off?"

They told him to jump. "All right; good-by." Shears said casually as he leaped to his death.

142

THE ROAD TO HELL: Cyrus Skinner was led down this main street of Hellgate to the corral where he was hanged.

THE GATE TO HELL: The corral fence which, with a timber leaning over it, served as a gallows for the hanging of Cyrus Skinner and several other desperadoes. The barn was once Boldt's Saloon.

THREE-STATE HOUSE: This house never has been moved, yet boundary changes have placed it in Oregon, Washington and Montana territories.

HOMEMADE HOME: Early houses in Montana were entirely hand made: logs notched to hold together without nails; sod roofs instead of shingles; and hand-hewn planks for doors and window sashes.

FIRST STORE IN MONTANA

Higgins and Worden's Store carried general merchandise. Display space may have been scanty, but Higgins and Worden's had a monopoly.

HELLGATE CANYON: The ancient highway of Indians to and from the buffalo country.

ST. MARY'S MISSION AND FORT OWEN

[51] Basing point: Missoula, Montana. Take U. S. Highway 93, 28.5 mi. south from Missoula to junction with a gravel road. Take gravel road across the Bitterroot River bridge 0.5 mi. to Fort Owen. Continue 1 mi. on to Stevensville. St. Mary's Mission is near the south end of town.

The Bitterroot Valley is particularly beautiful at this point, with St. Mary's Peak looming up as background for the mission.

EARLY missionaries had to be dexterous and resourceful, for anything could happen.

Father Pierre Jean DeSmet and six companions founded St. Mary's Mission in the spring of 1841. As the mission was being completed, an Indian worker recalled the prophecy made a few years before by a 13-year-old native girl named Mary. "Listen to the Black Robes when they come," she had said on that very spot, ". . . they will build the house of prayer where I am dying."

Crops as well as religion were introduced to the Indians. The next spring Father DeSmet planted potatoes, oats and wheat. That fall Montana's first crops of each were harvested. When Father Anthony Ravalli came to the mission in 1845, he and Father DeSmet built Montana's first gristmill.

The energetic DeSmet was always on the move from one mission to another, then East, then back again. It was said the total mileage of his journeys during those days of difficult travel equalled eight times the distance around the world. A strong man, he had unlimited courage. Once when threatened by an Indian he knocked the tomahawk from the aggressor's hand and threw him to the ground. Thrashing the man with a riding whip, Father DeSmet secured his promise to behave.

Father Ravalli had equal courage and talent. A physician, he treated his followers. An artist, he painted the altar and carved the statues of wood. Blacksmith and carpenter, he built much of the mission. One night as he sat in his cabin two Indians, Pascal and Charles, aimed a wavering gun at him through the window. That time he was probably thankful they were drunk, for the shot missed him and embedded itself in the log walls of the house.

Traders and trappers liked to winter in the pleasant climate of the Bitterroot Valley. Idling there, they demoralized the Indians. The priests remonstrated with the idlers, who angrily incited the Indians against the Black Robes. It became necessary to close the mission as such in 1850. Major John Owen bought the building and around it built Fort Owen.

With the closing of the church, Father Ravalli went away on other duties. Re-

PLACE OF WORSHIP: The St. Mary's Church with St. Mary's Peak as a background.

FATHER RAVALLI'S HOME

turning in 1866 he constructed a new church near Fort Owen, where he stayed until his death, October 2, 1884.

FORT OWEN

Later the most prominent trade center in the Bitterroot Valley, Fort Owen was founded by Major John Owen in 1850. In all of Montana only Fort Benton exceeded it in importance. Major Owen bought buildings from the Catholics at St. Mary's Mission and built some of his own. Here fur men obtained supplies, farmers sold their food, and stagecoaches left their precious loads. Major Owen and Sam Caldwell found gold near the fort in 1852, one of the first discoveries of the rich metal in Montana soil.

Harassed by Blackfeet Indians, Owen was forced to leave the Bitterroot. He returned to his fort with Governor Stevens of Washington Territory.

Stevens spent some time in the valley with Mullan, the road builder, at Cantonment Stevens, near Fort Owen. The little community that grew up there was named Stevensville, after the governor.

Road agent "Whisky" Bill Graves hid out at Fort Owen during the winter of 1864. The vigilantes dispatched three men to get him. A pistol pointed at his chest, Graves made no resistance. He was seated on a horse behind a vigilante. A rope was flung over a tree branch, and the knot adjusted around his neck. "Good-by, Bill," the vigilante said, digging his spurs into the horse. The horse lunged forward, and Whisky Bill was dead.

TRADING POST: Fort Owen, built and used for the fur trade by Major John Owen.

COZY?

The interior of one of the rooms in Fort Owen.

THE LEGEND OF
THE MEDICINE TREE

[52] Basing point: Missoula, Montana. Take U. S. Highway 93 south, past Hamilton and the little town of Darby, 76.4 mi. to the Medicine Tree. The well-marked tree is large and on the left side of the road.

This trip through the Bitterroot Valley follows closely the route of the Lewis and Clark Expedition.

CEREMONIAL DANCES and tribal rituals of the Salish Indians were performed under this medicine tree for generations. Here, on their annual pilgrimage to the Bitterroot Valley, the tribesmen made their invocations and hung offerings to the Great Spirit.

A ram horn was stuck into the tree in early days. On the mountainside back of the tree are several rocks resembling the profiles of Indian faces. From these facts, the legend of the tree was concocted.

There was a ram, a mountain sheep, who killed all who passed on the trail between the Bitterroot Valley and Rosses Hole. A coyote, clever as all his kind, taunted the ram about his strength. To show his power the ram charged the tree, impaling a horn in the trunk. The wily coyote killed him with a knife. Cutting off the ram's head, he threw it against the mountainside. Blood splashed about, coloring the rocks and leaving smears which looked like faces.

**THE
MEDICINE
TREE**

HAPPY HUNTING GROUND: Nez Perce graves at the west fork of the Bitter-root River.

THE BATTLE OF THE BIG HOLE

[53] Basing point: Missoula, Montana. Take U. S. Highway 93, 96.9 mi. to junction with State Highway 36 on Gibbon's Pass. Take gravel road to the left 19 mi. to the Big Hole Battlefield.

Chief Joseph and his Nez Perce band withdrew through this valley, pursued, unknown to them, by Colonel Gibbon and his men. The pass is named after Gibbon.

EVEN AS Pile of Clouds, their medicine man, urged them to press on, warning his tribesmen of his ominous dreams that "death was approaching," the Nez Perce relaxed their vigilance.

They were tired of war. There had been the White Bird Battle, the fighting at Cottonwood, the Rains Massacre and the Clearwater conflict, as well as minor skirmishes. They believed General O. O. Howard's pursuing troops had been left far behind when they crossed the Continental Divide into the Big Hole Basin.

The horses were turned loose to feed on the rich, plentiful grasses. The young men went on hunting parties. The women made comfortable lodges in the pleasant meadow, while the children caught fish in the river. Songs and celebration continued around the campfires far into the night. "War," they agreed, "is quit."

They could not know that General Howard, realizing he was outdistanced, had telegraphed Colonel John Gibbon at Fort Shaw, Helena. Accordingly Gibbon with 146 men of the 7th Infantry and 45 volunteers from Missoula and the Bitterroot Valley, was hot in pursuit of the Nez Perce.

About noon August 8, 1877, lieutenants Bradley and Jacobs, somewhat in advance of the main body, climbed a high tree. From this vantage they watched the activities in the Indian village and sent word back to Gibbon that the Nez Perce had been located.

Five miles from the Indian encampment the troops paused to eat and rest until dark. Quietly, in the twilight, they moved on. Laboring through dense timber, wading through swamps, and climbing over and under fallen trees, they sighted the Nez Perce campfires about two in the morning. Occasionally they would see a squaw dart from one of the lodges, pile fuel on the fires, and warm herself before returning to her buffalo robes.

As day broke, the troops were in position to attack. A lone Indian riding out to bring in the horses discovered them. Before he could cry a warning, he and his horse were shot. This was the signal for attack. The soldiers, charging across the creek and into the upper end of the camp, shot into the wigwams, killing the sleep-drugged occupants as they staggered out.

BIG HOLE BATTLEFIELD: The Indian encampment was among the willows in the foreground and extended upstream to the right. After the fight in the camp the troops were driven across the river and encircled on the bench among the pines.

Lieutenant Bradley and his men were the first to attack. He had been the first to discover the bodies of Custer's men on the Little Big Horn a year before. Perhaps he felt impelled to settle the score. But as he charged into a thicket an Indian, taking careful aim, killed him instantly.

As Captain Logan's men splashed over the stream, Logan killed a warrior with his revolver. The brave's squaw grabbed the gun and, firing at close range, wounded the captain. "I saw him . . . crawling like a drunken man . . . I struck him with my war club," said Yellow Wolf.

Most of the Indians, taken by surprise, had fled unarmed into the willow thickets. White Bird and Joseph rallied them, White Bird shouting: "Why are we retreating? Since the world was made brave men have fought for their women and children . . . Now is our time to fight."

The soldiers began to fire the lodges of the Nez Perce. Silhouetted against the red flames they made excellent targets for the Indians. Up from the lower camp came armed warriors, charging into the midst of the troops. Furiously fighting hand to hand, they forced the soldiers to give way. As the troops fled, the Nez Perce, greatest marksmen of all the American Indians, poured a galling fire into them.

Walitits, one of the three young men who had started the war by committing murders on Camas Prairie, was killed. (See "The Battle of White Bird Canyon.") Seizing his gun, his pregnant wife continued the fight until killed herself. She was found lying across his body as if to protect him.

Wahchumyus, whose name meant Rainbow, died in the battle. Pahkatas Owyeen, his closest friend, wept and began chanting his own death song. "This sun, this time, I am going to die. My Brother is killed and I am going with him."

The soldiers, out of the encampment, fought their way across the stream and gained a wooded point where they entrenched themselves. Indian sharpshooters surrounded them. Pahkatas Owyeen, still chanting his death song, crept near them, but was killed by Volunteer Otto Leifer. Some of the Indians were able to return to their lodges. Colonel Gibbon later wrote of the "wail of mingled grief, rage and horror which came from the camp when the Indians returned to it and recognized their slaughtered warriors, women and children."

The siege continued under the leadership of Chief Ollicut, Joseph's brother, who directed the battle and fought from behind a tree. Lieutenant English was fatally wounded. Sarpsus Ilp Pilp, another of the three who inaugurated the war, was killed. Strong Eagle, attempting to carry Sarpsus' body to safety, was wounded.

The Indians, shooting from behind the river bank, rocks and trees, kept the soldiers pinned down during the day. In the afternoon the Nez Perce fired the grass to burn out the soldiers. A change of wind brought a hoarse cheer from the men. The troops had no water, and ammunition was low.

Gibbon's men attempted to bring up a howitzer, which had not been able to travel as fast as the troops. The Indians, attacking the crew, killed several men and drove off the others. The gun they captured and dismantled.

154

The soldiers suffered from thirst. After dark some of them crawled to the river and brought back water. Lieutenant Woodruff's slain horse served as their food. Because of the accuracy of the Indians' aim, the troops did not dare to build a fire. They ate the horsemeat raw.

All through the following day the bitter fighting went on. The soldiers were encouraged by the arrival of a messenger with the news that General Howard was on his way with reinforcements. Later, his wagon train of supplies arrived. The Nez Perce women, children and old men had buried the dead, packed their belongings and escaped the first night. Learning through scouts of Howard's approach, the warriors singly drifted away to join the rest of their fleeing tribe. About 11 o'clock at night the remaining braves fired a final volley and silently left.

On August 11 the burial detail under Captain Comba buried the 29 soldier dead and cared for the 40 wounded, two of whom died. The detail counted 36 dead Indian warriors, and 53 dead Nez Perce women and children.

Those Nez Perce women who had taken refuge in nearby hills nursed their wounded before continuing the long retreat.

THE BEGINNING OF THE END: Sarpsus Ilp Pilp, one of the three young braves who started the Nez Perce War, was mortally wounded while fighting behind this tree.

END OF THE BEGINNER: Here Strong Eagle, carrying the dying Sarpsus, was wounded.

This was an old pros-
pect hole dug by Lut-
her Johnson ten years
before the battle.
Barnett Wilkerson, Nute
Davis, and Johnson
fought here.

Barnett Wilkerson, Nute Davis,
Luther Johnson, Volunteers
Entrenched Here

Timpoisman's
Who Chanted His War Song
Throughout The Battle

THE DISCOVERY OF GOLD AT LAST CHANCE GULCH

[54] Basing point: Helena, Montana. The main business district of Helena runs right up Last Chance Gulch.

Unlike Alder Gulch and the Grasshopper diggings, Last Chance Gulch did not become a ghost town. Quite the contrary, it became the capital of Montana. Many of the old buildings and bars still stand. A visitor in Helena should not fail to see the historical museum in the capitol building.

To THE Four Georgians, as to most prospectors, gold in distant diggings always glittered brighter than that at hand.

Why they were called the Four Georgians is inexplicable, since only two of them, John Cowan and John Crab, came from that state. Bob Stanley of London and D. J. Miller of California completed the quartet.

Since Alder Gulch, which proved to be the richest gold country in the world, hadn't yielded enough for them they were tempted to try their luck at Kootenai. They packed their equipment and toiled the many miles to Hellgate. Fabulous rumors ran like water through the early mining towns. Someone told them Kootenai was no good. The credulous Four changed their minds, deciding to prospect the Little Blackfoot River. How were they to know that Kootenai would bring fortunes in silver and lead to later prospectors?

Finding no gold on the Blackfoot, they worked their way eastward to gulch in Prickly Pear Valley. Although they found good color in several places, typically they continued their wanderings in quest of wealthier ground.

When their toiling and panning yielded nothing, they began to regret having left Prickly Pear Valley. With the eternal hope of the gold seeker, they turned back toward what they laughingly called Last Chance Gulch.

Arriving in Prickly Pear Valley on July 14, 1864, the Four Georgians tried a few prospects after supper. As they held nuggets in their hands and saw the gold dust in the ground they knew their last chance was a good one.

Cowan and Crab went to Alder Gulch the next morning for supplies and equipment, leaving Stanley and Miller to hold the claims. When they reached town, their story of a new strike caused wild excitement among the other prospectors. There was gold in Prickly Pear Valley! Many a miner shook off the dirt of Alder Gulch, the richest ground in the world, to rush to the new fields.

OVERLOOKING THE LAST CHANCE: A view of Helena and the Prickly
Pear Valley.

FORT BENTON

[55] Basing point: Great Falls, Montana. Go north 45 mi. on State Highway 29 to town of Fort Benton. The Old Fort Park is on Main Street, facing the Missouri River.

WHEN ALEXANDER CULBERTSON established what he at first called Fort Lewis at the Great Falls of the Missouri River, he was after beaver.

Representing the American Fur Company, Culbertson founded the fort in 1846. Temporary buildings were later torn down in favor of adobe structures. There was little timber in the vicinity, but the soil lent itself well to the making of bricks. Honoring Senator Thomas Benton of the State of Missouri, Culbertson renamed the fort in 1850.

The fort, 250 feet square with bastions at two corners, had no stockade. All the buildings faced the center, with the outer wall forming the backs of the structures. There were two gates on the river side of the fort.

Beaver were getting scarce. The fort, by 1850, was becoming more important to gold seekers than to fur traders. At the head of Missouri River navigation, as well as at the eastern end of the Mullan Road, Fort Benton saw pioneers and prospectors push off for the gold fields or for the extreme Northwest.

Several thousand Indians, mainly the truculent Blackfeet, lived in the vicinity of the fort. Their war and hunting parties had always used the ford in front of the fort to cross the river. The government, in 1869, stationed one company of the 7th Infantry in the fur company buildings to protect the citizens.

Although fighting was a hobby as well as a vocation with the Blackfeet, there were no general outbreaks. Soldiers were sent to the Blackfoot reservation with the body of a Gros Ventre who had been killed by Piegans. Another group went out to secure the bodies of two white whiskey traders, slain by the Assiniboines. Now and then detachments were sent in search of horses stolen by the Indians. The prevention of the illicit sale of liquor to the tribesmen also occupied the troops' time.

MUD TO ADOBE, ADOBE TO DUST: Part of the original wall at old
Fort Benton.

FORT BENTON ON THE MISSOURI

CHIEF JOSEPH'S LAST FIGHT AT BEAR PAW

[56] Basing point: Great Falls, Montana. Take State Highway 29, 156.7 mi. north to Havre. Go east on U. S. Highway 2, 21.7 mi. to Chinook. Turn right (south) from Central Avenue in Chinook onto dirt road, 16 mi. to the battlefield.
The Bear Paw Mountains are low, appearing to be hills rather than mountains.

AFTER MANEUVERING, fighting and retreating for nearly 2,000 miles, the Nez Perce were trapped at Bear Paw.

Leaving Yellowstone Park, Young Joseph and his band struck north toward the Canadian line. At Canyon Creek, north of the Yellowstone, they skirmished with Colonel Sturgis and his troops. Driving the troops back they continued their rapid, grueling trek northward.

They stopped just short of their goal. Exhaustion probably had something to do with it. Too, they were close to the Canadian border, and believed the troops were many miles behind.

Their scouts had not discovered General Nelson A. Miles and troops from the post on Tongue River, who were moving in a northeasterly direction to cut them off.

The Nez Perce were asleep in their lodges when General Miles' 7th Cavalry charged. One officer was humming "What Shall the Harvest Be?" Awakened by the thunder of the horses' hooves, the Indians alerted. As they approached the camp the cavalry were driven off by a hot fire. When the 5th Infantry moved up a bitter fight ensued. The Indians' escape was prevented by the 2nd Cavalry, who had come around behind them.

Skillfully and bitterly the Nez Perce fought four days. Casualties mounted on both sides and heavy snows added to the general suffering. On October 4, 1877, with 26 of his people killed and 46 wounded, Chief Joseph sent his message of surrender by a scout to the white camp.

". . . I am tired of fighting. Our chiefs are killed. Looking Glass is dead, Too-hul-hul-sote is dead. The old men are all dead . . . He who led on the young men is dead . . . the children are freezing to death . . . I want time to look for my children . . . Maybe I shall find them among the dead. Hear me, my chiefs. I am tired: my heart is sick and sad. From where the sun now stands I will fight no more forever."

Riding out of the timber with bowed head the chief slowly approached General Miles and General Howard, who had joined the troops the night before. Dismounting, Joseph offered his rifle to his old enemy, Howard. Graciously Howard nodded toward Miles, who accepted the token of final defeat of War Chief Joseph.

164

WATERLOO FOR THE RED NAPOLEON: In the foreground, the monument to the Indian dead. Background, marker to the soldier dead.

HONOR ROLL

The plaque on the monument to the soldier dead.

GRASSHOPPER DIGGIN'S AT BANNACK

[57] Basing point: Butte, Montana. From Butte take U. S. Highway 91, 65.9 mi. to Dillon. From Dillon take State Highway 36, a gravel road going west of the town. Cross Beaverhead River and go 17 mi. to the junction of the highway with an unimproved road. Turn left, and go south 6 mi. to the crossroads on Grasshopper Creek. At crossroads, turn left 1 mi. to Bannack.

Montana's livestock business started in this section of the old West. Oregon Trailers found it easily accessible, many of them settling in the rich valley. Often the gold seekers of the 1860's gave up their search for gold in favor of the more secure cattle breeding.

THE PHILOSOPHY that gold is where you find it brought John White and his party from the East. After searching fruitlessly for it in California and Colorado, they went north to Montana.

Leaving their camp on the Beaverhead River July 28, 1862, they prospected a small stream later called Grasshopper Creek. Gold was everywhere. In the stream bed, among the willows at its edge, in the rock ledges of the hills, and among the sagebrush roots the stuff lay waiting the prospector's pan.

Soon the Grasshopper diggings became a boisterous, swashbuckling mining camp. Some men brought their families in over the dangerous, Indian-infested Bozeman Road. Prospectors came from everywhere: California, Colorado, Idaho and the East. Preying on them was the usual following of gamblers, dance-hall girls and gunmen

The first Montana territorial government session was held here, in a building only slightly more pretentious than the nearby saloon and honky-tonk. Bannack had the first jail in Montana, but in those days when murder was not considered much of a crime the jail was not overworked.

Skinner's Saloon became the headquarters of the road agents, a band of robbers under the leadership of Bannack's notorious Sheriff Henry Plummer. Gold was easy to find and easier to lose to a robber or the gaming table.

John White was murdered, as he kindled a fire in night camp, by a thief he and a friend were returning to justice.

In the next 14 years over 144 million dollars in gold was taken from the mountains and streams of Montana.

DREAMING OF THE PAST: Bannack and Grasshopper diggings as seen from Hangman's Gulch.

LICENSE AND LEGISLATURE: Cyrus Skinner's saloon and the hotel that housed the first Montana legislative session. Skinner was hanged at Hellgate for his crimes as a road agent.

HENRY PLUMMER, SHERIFF AND BANDIT LEADER

[58]

THE MOST paradoxical man the West has ever known, Henry Plummer, was leader of the infamous road agents at Bannack in the early 1860's. Suave, polished, a steel-nerved gambler, a respected officer of the law, Plummer was also a murderous gunman, well qualified to conduct the grisly affairs of the desperadoes who overflowed Bannack.

Plummer was a slender, lithe man of about 27 years. His good grooming, brilliant conversation and apparent education made him many friends.

Probably from Connecticut, he was first heard of in California. There he murdered a man whose wife he had seduced and killed another while quarreling over a prostitute. Jailed, he broke out and fled to Walla Walla in Washington Territory. Trouble there prompted him to move to Lewiston, Idaho, where the road agents first were organized. At Lewiston and Orofino Plummer indulged in an orgy of murder and robbery.

Moving on to Bannack he continued his exploits by killing a friend, Jack Cleveland, in a saloon gun fight. Shortly after Plummer was wounded in the forearm by Sheriff Hank Crawford of Bannack. Crawford was a brave man but a chary one. He knew the road agents would not let him survive in Bannack and he left. Inexplicably, Henry Plummer, the cutthroat, was elected Henry Plummer, Sheriff.

Under these conditions lawlessness was rife. Rough men, who preferred giving the command, "Hands up!" to doing hard work, organized into a band called the Road Agents because of their frequent interferences with stagecoach traffic on the roads. Their password was "I am innocent," their meeting place was often Pete Daley's ranch, their mark of distinction a special sailor's knot in their neckties and their leader was Henry Plummer.

Everyone had gold, and many were careless with it. When autumn approached, miners who had made their pile began planning to return home to the East. The Walla Walla express was robbed by masked highwaymen. A long series of robberies and murders began. Stagecoaches carrying gold were secretly marked by spies.

Over 100 ruthless murders were committed in the years 1862 and 1863. Uncounted treasure and unnumbered men disappeared, as the robberies and holdups reached unreckonable proportions.

Following the trial and hanging of George Ives at Nevada City, the honest men of the three camps, Bannack, Virginia City and Nevada City, organized the vigi-

HOTEL FOR HORSE THIEVES: In 1862 murder was considered by some an ancient and honorable profession, but horse thieves were jailed and hanged.

A LONG ROAD FOR SOME: Plummer, Stinson and Ray were led up this road on a cold January night in 1862 to be hanged.

lantes. Red Yager and Brown, outlaws, were hanged on Passamari Creek. Before he died Yager gave the vigilantes full details of the road agent organization and the names of its members.

On a Sunday evening at Bannack one group of vigilantes found ex-convict Ned Ray wrapped in buffalo robes, sleeping on a saloon card table. Another party surprised Buck Stinson and led him without opposition from a Mrs. Toland's cabin. The party detailed to arrest Plummer found him washing his face in his cabin. Unconcernedly he wiped his face and said calmly, "I'll be ready as soon as I get my coat." One vigilante averted possible disaster when he noticed the butt of Plummer's gun showing under the coat. Getting the road agent's coat for him, the vigilante at the same time secured his gun. Plummer paled but remained composed.

The meeting place agreed on by the three groups of vigilantes was a gallows in Hangman's Gulch erected the preceding summer by Plummer himself for the execution of a murderer named Horan.

On the way up the gulch Plummer recognized the leader's voice as that of his neighbor, Wilbur F. Saunders. He pleaded for his life, but Saunders told him, "It is useless for you to beg for your life . . . you are to be hanged . . . I cannot help it if I would."

Plummer, now in slavish terror, screamed at them to do anything but kill him. "Cut off my ears. Cut out my tongue and strip me this freezing night and let me go. I beg you to spare my life . . . Oh God, I am too wicked to die." According to a member of the party, "he became loathsome in his abject and abandoned cowardice."

At the gallows Ned Ray, struggling and screaming curses, was first to be hanged.

"There goes poor Ned Ray," said Stinson. A moment later he was dangling by Ray's side.

Requesting time to pray, Plummer was coldly told to do his praying on the gallows. Less ruffled now, he removed his necktie and tossed it to a friend to remember him by. Of his executioners he requested a "good drop," and they complied.

The bodies soon stiffened in the icy wind of the bitterly cold night. They were later cut down and buried by friends.

It is generally believed Plummer was buried near the gallows. Legend has it, however, that the doctor who had treated his wounded arm after the fight with Crawford was curious about the position of the bullet. Exhuming the body, he found the bullet against the elbow, worn bright by the movement of the arm. Plummer, the legend continues, was re-buried in an unmarked grave in the cemetery on the hill, and only Stinson and Ray are in the grave at the gallows.

WAY OF THE TRANSGRESSOR: Plummer himself built the gallows to hang a horse thief.

3-7-77! The grave of Plummer, Stinson and Ray, 3 feet wide, 7 feet long and 77 inches deep.

DISCOVERY OF GOLD
AT ALDER GULCH

[59] Basing point: Butte, Montana. Take U. S. Highway 10S 23 mi. to its junction with State Highway 41. Turn south along the route of the old Vigilante Trail 39.6 mi. to Pete Daley's Robber's Roost, a large log building on the east side of the road. From Robber's Roost go 14.9 mi. farther south to Nevada City. Virginia City is 1.2 mi. south of Nevada City. Boothill Cemetery is on a low butte 0.4 mi. to the left of the main street of Virginia City.

Mr. Bovey, the Montana history lover, is doing a magnificent job of restoring and repairing the original buildings of Virginia City, rather than constructing unreal replicas. These will house the many relics of early days he has collected.

IMPETUOUS BILL FAIRWEATHER was young when he came West. In the spring of 1863 he, Henry Edgar and two others started out on a prospecting trip from Bannack to the Yellowstone.

When they encountered hostile Indians, Bill performed some white man's magic. According to Henry Edgar, rattlesnakes would not bite Bill Fairweather. As the Indians approached he picked up two snakes, holding one on each arm. The awestruck Indians believed him to be a great medicine man.

Bill put the snakes into his shirt bosom as he and his partners were taken into the medicine lodge. There they were marched around the sacred medicine bush innumerable times. Good-natured Bill, losing patience as he paraded, pulled the bush up by its roots and whacked the medicine man over the head with it. Although some of the Indians were angered by this sacrilege, the old chief held them back. The prospectors were freed, but relieved of their horses. Only Bill, whose antics intrigued the Indians, was allowed to keep his mount. Dimsdale in his *Vigilantes of Montana* says, "Bill was crazy, but he made it work."

The party gave up their plans to go to Yellowstone. Starting back toward Bannack, they prospected here and there as they went. They were destitute, thanks to their meeting with the Indians. Even carefree Bill grew concerned about finances

One day while the others were getting dinner, Bill and Edgar left camp to try to find enough gold for tobacco money when they returned to Bannack. Picking at the rimrock while Edgar washed the gravel, Bill knew he had struck it rich. With all his optimism, he couldn't envisage the wealth he had discovered. Alder Gulch supplied the world with over 100 million dollars' worth of gold.

Even though Bill loved to hunt for gold he placed little value on it once it was his. Valley Tan, the popular whiskey of the mining camp, was more to his liking. Under its influence he would ride up and down the main street of Virginia City, tossing gold dust in the air for the sport of seeing the children and Chinamen clamber for it. Bill was a pauper when he died at the age of 39.

HE SOUGHT GOLD TO THROW AWAY: Bill Fairweather, discoverer of gold at Alder Gulch, died a pauper.

$100,000,000 TOBACCO MONEY: The diggings at Alder Gulch were first turned over by the shovels of the early miners, then reworked by Chinamen. Now giant dredges go down to bedrock.

VIRGINIA CITY, THE LAWLESS

[60]

WHEN THE news of Bill Fairweather's gold discovery reached Bannack a stampede for Alder Gulch got under way. Soon the area was dotted with tents, brush huts and hastily-built log cabins. Claims were staked along the whole 12 miles of the gulch

Judges were chosen and laws adopted. A controversy arose over naming the mining town. Southern sympathizers chose Varina, after Jefferson Davis' wife. The name did not sit well with the Northerners. Dr. Bissel, one of the miners' judges, substituted Virginia City. The compromise was acceptable to all concerned.

Within 90 days there were 10,000 people in Alder Gulch. The ample gold beckoned a more than ample retinue of gamblers and glittering dance belles. Almost every third building in Virginia City was a crowded saloon.

The miners' courts worked to some extent in civil cases, but made little attempt to settle fights or shooting scrapes. During the outdoor trial of one civil case, three road agents rode up to Deputy Dillingham and called him aside. Dillingham was the one honest deputy sheriff attending the trial. He previously had warned a stagecoach driver of a road-agent plan to rob him. The agents, Charley Forbes, Haze Lyons and Buck Stinson, fired on Dillingham simultaneously, murdering him in plain sight of the judge and jury.

Forbes, in a separate trial, was acquitted in a miners' court because of his youth and good appearance. Lyons and Stinson, convicted, were condemned to hang. The gallows were built and the graves dug. When pressure from the road agents brought about a new vote in the court they were acquitted. The powerless miners realized that some of the road agents voted as many as three times. A "For Rent" sign was posted over Stinson's and Lyons' unfilled graves.

The travesty left things wide open for the Innocents in Virginia city; Nevada City, two miles down the gulch; and Bannack.

ASLEEP IN THE SUN: Once the most exciting town in the West, Virginia City drowses away the hot afternoons.

TWILIGHT: Virginia City reposes peacefully in the dusk.

THE HANGING OF GEORGE IVES AT NEVADA CITY

[61]

SEARCHING in a clump of sagebrush for a grouse he had shot in the Passamari Valley, William Palmer, a hunter, found the bird had fallen on the frozen body of Nicholas Tiebault, nicknamed The Dutchman. He had obviously been robbed and murdered. It was December 17, 1863. The Dutchman had disappeared nine days before.

Indignation was rife in Virginia City and Nevada City. It was one thing to hold up stages and occasionally kill a man. That held a slight element of sporting chance. It was quite another thing to murder cold-bloodedly a hard-working boy like The Dutchman.

A miners' posse arrested George Ives as the murderer. Ives, one of the road agents who brought terror and death to highway travelers, was full of bravado. Blond, handsome and wicked, he joked as he rode with his captors. Growing merrier as they trotted along, the men took up Ives' suggestion that they race their mounts. After allowing the others to win several contests the prisoner spurred his horse to a wild gallop. It was two hours before his startled pursuers recaptured him.

Although Ives hoped for a trial by civil authorities in Virginia City where his influential cohorts would choose the jury, the men took him to Nevada City. A miners' court was organized the following day. During the three days of the trial a wagon served as the platform for Judge Don L. Byam. Another wagon held Ives, the lawyers and witnesses. The third evening the jury found George Ives guilty. It was growing dark when Prosecutor Wilbur Saunders moved that Ives be hanged.

A roar arose, the approval of the miners mixing with the curses and threats of the road agents. Guns clicked as the angry witnesses milled about.

To prevent his rescue by allies, the prisoner was encircled by a grim group of men who faced the crowd holding shotguns breast high, ready for action.

George Ives was hanged that night, December 21, 1863.

DEN OF THIEVES: Robbers' Roost, Pete Daley's ranch, favorite meeting place of the road agents.

COURTROOM: Open-air today as it was in 1863.

VIGILANTES AT VIRGINIA CITY

[62]

"WHILE we are here betting, those Vigilantes are passing sentence of death on us," Jack Gallagher remarked to another road agent as they gambled. Gallagher was more truthful than he knew. In a building not far from the saloon where the terrorists were gambling, the vigilantes were at that hour passing judgment on them.

The vigilance committee of five men from Virginia City and four from Bannack was formed during the trial of George Ives. It was patterned after the committee that had established order in California during the gold rush days.

Meetings were held in the loft of a livery stable in Virginia City. No one knows the exact origin of the secret sign, 3-7-77, which they adopted. It is thought it represented the dimensions of a grave three feet wide, seven feet long and 77 inches deep. The organization was created "for the purpose of arresting murderers and thieves and recovering stolen property." "Men do your duty," was their motto.

Their first action was to hang two road agents named Brown and Yager on Passamari Creek. The next agents to be hanged were Plummer, Stinson and Ray at Bannack.

At their meeting January 13, 1864, the vigilante executive committee decided to capture and hang Gallagher, Boone Helm, Frank Parish, Haze Lyons, George Lane and Bill Hunter.

The next morning they led Parish from a store where he was idling.

They found Gallagher in the "Shades," a saloon where he had gambled the night before.

Helm, the toughest of the lot, solemnly protested innocence when first caught. Finding his pretence useless, the road agent, whose crimes included cannibalism, started asking for whiskey.

Clubfoot George Lane calmly requested a minister.

Haze Lyons, the last of the five captured, was eating breakfast when caught. Offered a chance to complete it, he shook his head. His appetite was gone.

Bill Hunter, the sixth condemned man, had escaped during the night.

Lyons was taken to Pfouts store. Parish, Lane, Gallagher and Helm were there ahead of him.

An unfinished building was selected as the execution spot, with a rafter as the gallows.

As the nooses were being adjusted, Pfouts asked if the guilty men had any last

178

STRANGLERS' RENDEZVOUS: The vigilantes met in the loft of this livery stable.

THEY SINNED: The graves of Parish, Gallagher, Helm, Lyons and Lane were marked because of a bet; other road agents rest in the rocky soil in nameless graves.

requests. "How do I look in this necktie, boys?" asked Gallagher who alternately cursed, grinned and cried. On being asked again, he requested and received a drink of Valley Tan, a popular whiskey of the day.

"Every man for his own principles, three cheers for Jeff Davis," shouted Helm, "let her rip."

At the command "Men do your duty," the road agents were hanged one by one.

Since no markers were placed on the graves their location became uncertain as the years passed. An argument occurred eventually between Wilbur Saunders and Ariel Davis, two of the execution party. George Lane was exhumed. His clubfoot was removed and taken to the museum at Virginia City. The graves were relocated and marked with pine boards, later to be replaced by metal markers.

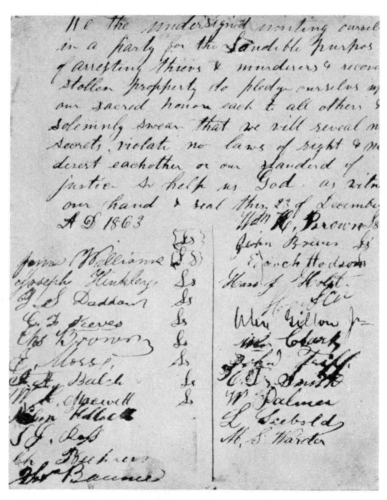

**A photographic copy of the original
vigilante oath.**

HANGMANS BUILDING
— 1864 —
SEE THE ORIGINAL GALLOWS 3-7-77
USED BY VIGILANTES
HANGED (1864) HERE.
~~GEORGE LANE~~
FRANK PARISH ~ HAZE LYONS.
JACK GALLAGHER-BOON HELM.

OFFICE
Va DIST
WATER CO.

END OF THEIR ROPE: When this building was yet unfinished the rafters
served as a gallows.

Right: Rope burns still show on the rafter.

COLTER'S RACE FOR LIFE AT THREE FORKS

[63] Basing point: Three Forks, Montana. Take U. S. Highway 10, 2.2 mi. east. Take gravel road on the left to where the Gallatin unites with the Madison and Jefferson rivers to form the Missouri River.

The Missouri Fur Company sent trappers to establish a trading post at the three forks. Driven off by Blackfeet they went across the Divide to establish Fort Henry, first white habitation west of the Rockies.

To THE INDIANS, explorer John Colter must have seemed fabulously indestructible.

As Lewis and Clark worked their way homeward down the Missouri River, Colter, a member of their party's two-year expedition, wanted still more adventure. Finding two young men who were going hunting up the Yellowstone, Colter requested and was given permission by Lewis and Clark to join the hunt. "The example of this man," Clark remarked, "shows how easily a man may be weaned from the habits of civilization to the ruder though scarcely less fascinating manners of the woods."

Colter traded, trapped and explored in the region that later became Yellowstone Park. He assisted in the preparation of many early maps.

In the spring of 1808 Colter with another member of the Lewis and Clark party named John Potts was trapping in the vicinity of the three forks of the Missouri River. Blackfeet Indians appeared on the shore as the two men paddled down the river in their canoe. The Indians commanded Colter and Potts to come to them. Having no choice, they started to oblige. Colter stepped out of the canoe, but the terrified Potts pushed out into the stream. As he raised his gun to shoot he was instantly struck down by Blackfeet arrows.

Completely at their mercy, John Colter waited while the Indians discussed how they should prolong his killing. Stripping him of his clothes, they gave him a head start in a race for his life. Colter was a tough man. He outran the whole swift group with the exception of one brave. Colter stopped suddenly, throwing the Indian off stride. Grasping the faltering pursuer's spear, Colter stabbed him to death. Apparently this interval of rest for his legs refreshed him and he sprinted for the river. The remaining Indians were far enough behind to enable him to leap into the river, swim down a way, and dive under a log jam to conceal himself. The frustrated Indians searched for hours before giving up.

Naked, barefoot, hungry and without weapons, Colter climbed out of the river. Picking his way through barbed cactus and sagebrush of the torrid desert he struggled through the Gallatin Valley into the Yellowstone Valley. Traveling nearly 200 miles, he reached the fort at the mouth of the Big Horn River. There he arrived in quite good health, although heavily sunburned and doubtlessly hungry.

Composed, calm John Colter then resumed his exploring and fur trading.

THREE FORKS: Here the Madison, Gallatin and Jefferson rivers join to form the Missouri River.

FORT ELLIS IN THE
GALLATIN VALLEY

[64] Basing point: Bozeman, Montana. Take U. S. Highway 10, 3 mi. east to monument on left (north) side of road.

The stone on which the bronze plaque is mounted once held the sundial near the officers' quarters of the old fort.

The actual site of the fort is now used by Montana State College as an experiment station. None of the original buildings remain.

GUARDING the Gallatin Valley from Indian attacks, which some feared, some desired and some imagined, was the chief task of Fort Ellis. Also, friction between the Sioux from the east and the miners at Bannack, Virginia City and Helena made a garrison necessary.

The site was selected by Captain E. W. Clift in 1867. On August 27 of that year two companies of the 13th Infantry arrived to establish the fort. In 1869 two companies of the 2nd Cavalry were added to the garrison.

Military escorts for the survey parties of the Northern Pacific Railroad were provided by Fort Ellis. Settlers in the Gallatin Valley were afforded protection from roving Indians going to the buffalo lands.

Because of their natural fear of the Indians the settlers often fancied troubles where none existed. Sometimes their imagination led to very real consequences. One expedition of whites, the Yellowstone Wagon Road and Prospecting Expedition, was rumored to have deliberately provoked attack to give the military a chance to subdue the Indians completely. By eliminating Indian resistance, they hoped to open the Big Horn and Yellowstone valleys to trade from the Gallatin Valley.

As expected, the expedition was assaulted by the Indians. Six members of the party were killed and eight wounded before troops from Fort Ellis could rescue them. The foray obviously had no decisive effect on making the valleys safe.

JOHN M. BOZEMAN,
TRAIL BLAZER

[65] Basing point: Bozeman, Montana. From Bozeman post office take U. S. Highway 10, 0.6 mi. east to entrance to a park. Turn right 0.2 mi. to cemetery entrance. Continue straight ahead 0.1 mi., then turn right 0.2 mi. Turn right again for 150 feet. The Bozeman grave is on the right in the Nelson Story plot.

To reach the spot where Bozeman was killed, take Highway 10, 26 mi. to Livingston on the east side of Bozeman Pass. Continue east 12.8 mi. to highway sign designating the spot.

JOHN M. BOZEMAN of Georgia was one of the many men the gold fields lured to adventure.

Like his father who left wife and family to seek gold in California in '49, Bozeman headed for the Colorado gold fields in 1858, leaving his wife and three children.

Finding others had beat him to the best diggings in Colorado, he went on to Bannack, Montana. At Bannack he tried his hand at mining, but the tiresome work soon bored him.

All men were searching for fortunes in those days, and Bozeman looked about for a less tedious and quicker method of obtaining his. He and another man, John Jacobs, planned and laid out a shorter, more direct route to the Montana gold fields. During the next few years he guided wagon trains and gold seekers over his new route.

Bozeman with a companion, Tom Cover, started down the Yellowstone toward Fort C. F. Smith on April 17, 1867. Ordinarily fearless and confident, he seemed to have a presentiment on this trip. The next night he asked a friend with whom he and Cover camped to take his place on the journey to the fort. Apparently the friend refused, and April 20 found Cover and Bozeman in noon camp up a little ravine just off the Yellowstone.

Sighting Indians, Bozeman thought them friendly Crows and allowed them to approach. The Indians came up with outstretched hands, saying, "Apsarake apsarake," meaning "We are Crows." They shook hands with Bozeman who suddenly turned to Cover and said, "I am fooled. They are Blackfeet."

One of the Indians fired on Bozeman. He did not fall, although the bullet entered his right breast and went clear through him. As he tried to rush the Indian another shot killed him instantly.

Cover, at the same time, was shot through the shoulder. Finding his gun out of order, he started to dash away. When he had fled about 50 yards he managed to fix his gun. Turning, he fired a shot which he later claimed killed one of the Indians. He escaped on foot, swam the Yellowstone, and walked 30 miles to the camp of friends.

Bozeman was buried where he fell. Later his remains were taken to the town named for him. After a public ceremony, he was reinterred in the city cemetery.

186

"I AM FOOLED . . ."

Above: The gulch where Bozeman and Cover met the Blackfeet. *Right:* Bozeman's grave in the cemetery of the town that was given his name.

CLARK'S TRIP DOWN THE YELLOWSTONE

[66] Basing point: Big Timber, Montana. Go east on U. S. Highway 10, 0.7 mi. to monument commemorating Rivers Across Camp of Lewis and Clark.

The formation captioned "Flat Top" shown on the opposite page is a number of miles farther down the river. It is included here because Clark mentions it in his *Journal*.

WHEN CAPTAIN CLARK's section of the Lewis and Clark Expedition reached this portion of the Yellowstone River, July 14, 1806, they noted in the *Journal*, "The River was now becoming more divided by islands and a number of small creeks fell into it from both sides." Finding two streams joining the river nearly opposite one another, they named the northern stream Otter and the southern Beaver. Although they found deer and elk scarcer, buffalo were beginning to be more plentiful.

In the river bottom they observed an Indian fort, which they described as about 50 feet in diameter and five feet high. It was built of lapped-over logs and covered with bark on the outside. Sacajawea told them such entrenchments were frequently constructed by Minnetarees and other Indians warring with the Shoshones.

Near this camp a Mr. Gibson was injured seriously by falling on a splinter of wood. This accident delayed the party, making it necessary to build dugout canoes to continue their trip. Indians stole 24 of their horses during the pause.

"Nor were the Indians the only plunderers," the *Journal* continues, "for in the night wolves . . . stole the greater part of the dried meat from the scaffold. The wolves which constantly attend the buffalo were here in great numbers."

FLAT TOP: This peculiar formation attracted the attention of Clark. His expedition camped near here on the Yellowstone River.

THE BLACKFEET INDIANS
AND THE THOMAS MASSACRE

[67] Basing point: Big Timber, Montana. Go east 14.3 mi. on U. S. Highway 10. The Thomas grave is just outside the fence on the south side of the road. There is a wooden highway marker.

Big Timber, originally an old stage station on the Bozeman Road, is the center of the principal dude-ranching areas of the West. In the summer cars from every state in the Union can be seen on its streets.

THE HANDSOME, splendidly-built Blackfeet Indians were exceptionally antagonistic to the influx of the white man. Their enmity toward the Long Knives, as they called the traders, extends back before the records of history.

Not native to Montana, the Blackfeet were probably of Algonquin stock, originating in the region north of the Great Lakes. About the middle of the 18th century they moved southward and westward. Although at that time they did not use horses, they were excellent buffalo hunters. They arranged traps called *pishkuns* at the bases of cliffs. Shouting and waving their robes, they would stampede the buffalo over the cliffs to destruction in the traps.

Learning the use of horses, they became dexterous riders. Their contact with British traders led to their early familiarity with firearms. These abilities together with their superior physiques made formidable warriors of them. The scourge of the frontier, they were almost constantly at war with the Crows, Nez Perce, Shoshones and other tribes of the region as well as with the whites.

Although Lewis and Clark were the first white men many western Indians had ever seen, the explorers experienced no Indian trouble until they ran into Blackfeet on their return trip. The Indians attempted to steal horses from the Lewis and Clark party. Two Blackfeet were killed in the ensuing fight.

Many others tasted the bitterness of Blackfeet hostility. In 1866 William Thomas and his eight-year-old son Charles, of Illinois, and a man named Schultz, from Ontario, headed West from Fort Laramie, Wyoming. Traveling with a wagon train, their goal was Montana's Gallatin Valley. During the first part of the journey they were escorted by soldiers detailed to build Fort C. F. Smith on the Big Horn River.

After the troops stopped to build the fort, somehow Schultz, Thomas and the boy were separated from the rest of the wagon train. They continued alone. A few weeks later their bodies were found beside the road, slain by the Blackfeet. The discovering party dug a grave and buried them.

190

GONE WEST: The Bozeman Road, the Oregon Trail, the Mullan Road and the California Cut-off all have many such tragic spots, most of them unmarked and unknown.

SACAJAWEA'S SON, BAPTISTE, AND THE NAMING OF POMPEY'S PILLAR

[68] Basing point: Billings, Montana. Take Highway 10, 29.8 mi. east. The rock is on the left (north) side of the road across an open field near the river. The Montana Highway Department has identified it with a signboard on the road.

Here one can almost see the smoke signals curling upward. Generations of Indians used Pompey's Pillar as a communication agency. The Pillar was their lookout, their smoke-writing base, and their tablet on which they carved messages. Fur traders and pioneers, too, found the soft sandstone useful to hew information for those who followed.

Clark's name is preserved by an iron grill to protect it from modern vandals and, unfortunately, photographers.

THE SON of Sacajawea gave his nickname to Pompey's Pillar.

The baby Baptiste was with his mother on the Lewis and Clark Expedition. The infant was popular with Captain Clark who liked to call him Pompey. Pomp is the Shoshone Indian word for chief.

After a day's travel by boat down the Yellowstone, Captain Clark landed on the afternoon of July 25, 1806, to "examine a very remarkable rock situated in an extensive bottom two hundred and fifty paces from the shore," according to his *Journal*. "The Indians have carved figures of animals and other objects on the sides of the rock," he continued, "and on the top are raised two piles of stones . . . The north side of the river for some distance is here surrounded by jutting romantic cliffs succeeded by rugged hills, beyond which the plains are again open . . . and the whole country was enlivened by herds of buffalo, elk and wolves."

After enjoying the view from the 200-foot tower, Clark carved his name in the stone and called the rock Pompey's Pillar.

As Baptiste grew older Clark begged permission to provide for his education. Sacajawea agreed and the boy was schooled in St. Louis. In 1830 at the age of 25 he joined his tribesmen, apparently living a typical Indian existence until his death in 1885.

CLARK'S SIGNATURE ON POMPEY'S PILLAR: All sides of this sandstone rock are covered with names, dates, messages and Indian pictographs, but the most distinguished signature is Clark's for which the Northern Pacific Railroad has provided an iron grill to guard against vandalism.

POMPEY'S PILLAR: "This rock I ascended and from its top had a most extensive view in every direction," Clark said, adding that the Indians had made two piles of stone on top of this tower. "The nativs have ingraved on the face of this rock the figures of animals &c near which I marked my name and the day of the month & year," which was Friday, July 25, 1806.

CUSTER'S BATTLE ON THE LITTLE BIG HORN

[69] Basing point. Billings, Montana. From junction with U. S Highway 10 take Highway 87, 49.8 mi. east to Hardin, then 13.3 mi. south to the Crow Agency. Continue 1.6 mi. Turn left 1 mi. to the Custer monument. The gravel road continues straight ahead about 4 mi. to Reno Hill.

The territory from Billings to the Custer Battlefield is profuse in Indian legend and history. Here great herds of buffalo roved. Near Billings is the Inscription Cave, its walls enriched with ancient Indian writing.

THE GREAT Sioux uprising of 1876 was due primarily to the violation of a treaty by the whites. As the Nez Perce regarded their sacred Wallowa Lake, so the Sioux prized their Black Hills hunting ground. When gold was discovered there, prospectors threw the treaty to the four winds and invaded the country with pick and shovel.

The Sioux left their reservation and united their various bands: the Brules, the Sans Arcs, the Minneconjous, the Uncpapas and the Ogallallas. Another badly abused tribe, the Cheyennes, joined the Sioux on the warpath.

In the spring of 1876 generals Crook, Gibbon and Terry, with their troops, began a campaign to punish the Sioux and drive them back to their reservation. The Indians were believed to be in the vicinity of the Big Horn River.

In an attempted pincers movement, General Gibbon was to come east from Fort Ellis, Montana; Crook to come north from Wyoming; and Terry, with Lieutenant Colonel (ex-Civil War General) George A. Custer and the 7th Cavalry, were to come west from Fort Abraham Lincoln at Mandan, North Dakota.

On the morning of May 15, their guidons snapping briskly in the breeze, the 7th Cavalry paraded at Fort Abraham Lincoln. After the review, as the troubled wives and sweethearts watched the regiment move out of sight over the hills, a strange and ominous mirage occurred. The columns of the 7th seemed to leave the earth and march away into the sky.

THE PLAN

Not having heard from Crook, Terry and Custer halted the march at the Rosebud River and held council. It was decided Terry would continue up the Yellowstone to the mouth of the Little Big Horn River, there to join Gibbon and his command and proceed up the Little Big Horn. Custer was to go up the Rosebud, swing over the hills to the Little Big Horn, meeting Terry and Gibbon. The forces were then to combine in an attack on the Sioux.

June 22, as Custer's troops were preparing to march up the Rosebud, many of them took the opportunity to write their families. The premonitory letters of these

FOXHOLES: The rifle pits on Reno Hill. Water volunteers used the ravine at the right. Reno's first attack on the Indian encampment was made about where the road shows in the center of the picture.

SNIPER'S NEST

An Indian on top of this butte using a long-range rifle killed three troopers and wounded two.

veterans, who ordinarily relished the thought of battle, and their conversation among themselves indicated a strange foreboding.

Scouting carefully as they went, the regiment proceeded up the Rosebud River. Soon they saw evidence that a large Indian party was ahead of them. Custer did not know that the Sioux, stirred to fighting pitch by Sitting Bull, their medicine man, had administered a heavy defeat to General Crook on June 17. The Indians, ably led by their war chiefs Crazy Horse, Gaul, Fast Bull, Red Bear and Two Moons, had forced Crook to retreat thus preventing his joining the other forces.

Custer's troops, after a brief rest on the night of June 24, cut across the hills westward toward the Little Big Horn. At dawn of June 25 Custer climbed the highest hill in the vicinity. With field glasses he discovered a seemingly endless Sioux encampment on the far shore of the river.

Custer ordered Captain Benteen with two troops to scout the south and west. Major Reno with three troops was ordered to advance toward the upper end of the encampment and attack from there. Captain MacDougal with his troop was directed to come along behind with the pack train and ammunition. Custer himself, with 231 men, planned to swing out to the right and pitch into the lower end of the camp.

RENO'S ATTACK

At a swift trot, Major Reno and his command splashed across the Little Big Horn, advancing on the south end of the encampment in columns of four. The Indians fired on them. The horses of three of the troopers became unmanageable and stampeded straight into the horde of Indians.

Realizing a charge into such a throng would be disastrous, Reno commanded his men to dismount and fight on foot. When the Indians swarmed around them, Reno ordered his troops to fall back and take up a position in a grove of cottonwood timber on a bend in the river. Hundreds of Indians were riding in a half circle, firing from under their horses' necks and then dashing away. Casualties occurred right and left among the dismounted cavalrymen. Bloody Knife, one of Custer's Indian scouts, was shot through the head. His brains spattered over Major Reno.

Although the position was a good one, the major, seemingly in a panic, commanded his men to mount. Two of his three troop commanders heard the order. The third, Lieutenant McIntosh, knew of the order only after he saw the other two troops fleeing madly upstream to find a place to ford the river.

All discipline had vanished. The frantically riding cavalrymen broke through the Indians, jumped their horses over a five-foot bank into the river and plunged across. Gaining the other side, they scrambled up a narrow trail in the hills to the east.

Reaching the top of the hill, the troopers rallied and dug in. The number of Indians kept increasing. One hostile, gaining the top of a higher hill, killed several soldiers in the rifle pits with an accurate, long-range rifle.

196

MONUMENT ON RENO HILL

The wounded were cared for in a hollow near here.

WHERE GRAPES OF WRATH WERE STORED: Custer tried to ford the Little Big Horn River here. Sergeant Butler was killed and Custer's men driven back by Indians concealed in the ravine.

Captain Benteen and his two troops. having found no Indians on their march, were returning when they met Sergeant Kanipe who was riding hard toward Mac-Dougal's pack train with a message from Custer: "Come on quick . . . a big Indian camp." Soon Trumpeter Martin, on a horse spouting blood from a bullet wound, brought Benteen an urgent message from Custer's adjutant, Lieutenant Cook. "Benteen, come on. Big Village. Be quick. Bring packs. P.S. Bring pacs." The packs contained the extra ammunition Custer so urgently needed.

But from the west came the roar of the Reno battle. Benteen ordered his men to draw their revolvers. Charging up the bluffs at a gallop, they joined Major Reno's beaten and disorganized men on the hilltop. They fought for their lives the rest of the day. Heavy rifle fire was heard during the afternoon from the direction Custer had taken. The men on the hilltop were too occupied to do much more than wonder.

CUSTER'S MOVEMENTS

Custer and his men had moved rapidly down the east side of the Little Big Horn, screened from the Indians by an intervening ridge. Cutting squarely to the right, they rode to the top of a bluff from which they saw the great Indian encampment. Anxious for action, the troopers cheered. Some of the horses were nervous. As Sergeant Kanipe left with the message for MacDougal he heard Custer caution, "Hold your horses in. boys. There are plenty of them down there for us all." Trumpeter Martin related. "The last I saw of the command they were going down the ravine; the Gray Horse troop was in the center, and they were galloping."

Only the positions of the dead on the battlefield and the Indians tell the story from this point on.

Custer's men galloped down the ravine and approached the ford beyond which lay the village of Sans Arc Sioux. Indians were already across, hidden in the sagebrush and ravines. Custer's men were driven back.

The 7th retreated to the top of a long T-shaped ridge, dismounted and dug in as much as possible. Captain Keogh and his men held the ridge on the right, and Lieutenant Calhoun on the left. Crittenden manned the stem of the T.

"We were lying in the gullies behind sagebrush hillocks, but we kept creeping in closer all around the ridge," said a Sioux warrior.

The location of the graves indicate most of Keogh's men held their positions until death. Shooting arrows into the horses, the Indians succeeded in stampeding them. The horses overran Calhoun's men, creating confusion and dust. With this advantage. the hostiles stole in closer. Again the graves tell the story. Calhoun's men, after fighting bravely for a while, were overrun and fled in the direction of Custer's position at the base of the T. Many were killed at the bottom of a ravine just back of the ridge they had held. The rest were killed as they rushed up the opposite slope.

Custer and the remaining men made a last stand on the hilltop. The Indians, riding in an ever-tightening circle, demolished them.

THE FIRST TO FALL: Sergeant Butler's body was found here.

STILL HOLDING THE LINE: These probably were Captain Keogh's men.

The commands of Reno and Benteen, meanwhile, were pinned to the top of Reno Hill in the flaming afternoon sun. All were thirsty and exhausted; many were wounded.

The fighting on Reno Hill became fierce. Destruction of the entire force seemed inevitable, but twilight brought a welcome slackening of the attack. With darkness, the battle ceased.

The troopers lay shivering in the blackness on Reno Hill, overlooking the Little Big Horn. From below came the harsh shouts of the Indians celebrating their triumph.

At dawn the Indians resumed their attack. The troopers were out of water. Seventeen volunteered to make the steep descent to the river while others kept up a steady fire into the brush where the Indians were concealed. Although several volunteers were wounded, the men succeeded in bringing water back to the parched throats on the hilltop.

Early in the afternoon the Indians appeared to be burning the grass in the valley. Rifle fire on the hill lessened. The besieged men became aware that the warriors were leaving.

TERRY AND GIBBON APPROACH TOO LATE

On the morning of June 27, Lieutenant Bradley, scouting in advance of Terry and Gibbon's approaching column, discovered the carnage on Custer Hill. The only living creature on that bleak hill was Captain Keogh's dun-colored horse, Commanche, which was so badly wounded the Indians had not bothered to take him.

The bodies of General Custer and his brothers, Captain Tom Custer and civilian Boston Custer, lay close by some 30 of the troopers. The bodies of Custer's brother-in-law, Lieutenant James Calhoun, and his men lay farther out on the hill. All except Custer were mutilated and stripped of their clothing and valuables. Custer was untouched, except for three bullet wounds. All of the 231 men who rode with Custer were killed. A horse with 7th Cavalry equipment was found at the mouth of the Rosebud River, dead of a bullet wound, a month after the battle. If he was taken there by a 7th soldier, it indicates one man nearly escaped. Several bodies were never found.

Fifty-three of Reno's and Benteen's men were killed and 54 wounded. Some Indians named their loss at 30 to 35. Certainly their losses were comparatively light.

The men were buried where they fell. Each shallow grave was marked by a name on a slip of paper placed in an empty cartridge shell and jammed over a willow stake.

A year later wolves and coyotes had so scattered the remains that everything above ground was collected and buried in a common grave where the large monument stands.

Today white markers dot the hill. Relocating the graves was difficult, because many of the original markers had long since disappeared. They were accurately placed, however, by locating the spots where the grass, enriched by a soldier's life blood, grew taller.

THE GRASS GREW TALL: Lieutenant James Calhoun, Custer's brother-in-law, was killed here.

PANIC: When the Indians stampeded the horses, Calhoun's men apparently fled in mad confusion down the ravine at the right and up the slope where Custer was making his last stand.

CONFUSION AND DEATH: This picture is a reverse view of the picture immediately preceding.

THE HILLS OF THE LITTLE BIG HORN: This ridge forms the stem of the T that Custer selected for his last stand. It was held by Lieutenant Crittenden and his troop.

THEIR SOULS GO MARCHING ON: Here Custer and the remnants of his men fought the ever-tightening circle of Sioux and Cheyenne warriors.

THE SEVEN SUICIDES: An Indian told of seven men who broke away and ran for the river but, finding themselves surrounded, turned their revolvers on themselves. The seven markers are shown in the exact center of the picture. The cluster of markers beyond were probably Lieutenant Smith's troop who lost their lives in a vain charge against the warriors.

WIVES OF THE 7th CAVALRY
AT FORT ABRAHAM LINCOLN

[70] Basing point: Mandan, North Dakota. Take State Highway 6, 4.5 mi. south to Fort Abraham Lincoln State Park.

Space does not permit the presentation in this book of the many spots of historic interest between the Custer battlefield and Mandan. These pages about Fort Abraham Lincoln, however, find their place because they seem a fitting sequel to the tragedy on the Little Big Horn.

ALL ITS former gaiety and sparkle left Fort Abraham Lincoln when an Indian scout brought the news of the Little Big Horn disaster to the wives of the 7th Cavalry.

A few months before the fort had vibrated with the friendly social life that was so accentuated in the tight, isolated circle of a post. Here in the Custer home officers and their wives had enjoyed the parties and gatherings of the popular lieutenant colonel and his wife, Elizabeth. Lieutenant Crittenden, Captain Keogh, Tom Custer, Lieutenant Calhoun and Lieutenant Sturgis had walked these roads. Enlisted men had danced here, supplied plays and entertainment here, married here.

Now desolation replaced all that pulsating life. Many wives of the 7th knew their husbands lay in shallow graves in the Little Big Horn country.

THE GAYEST HOME AT THE POST: Custer's house now lies in ruins with the other houses on officers' row.

FORT ABRAHAM LINCOLN: The 7th Cavalry was stationed here in the spring of 1876 just before leaving for the Little Big Horn Battle.

THE BATTLE OF WHITE BIRD CANYON

Alternate Route: Weiser, Idaho, to Seattle, Washington (See End Sheet Map)

[71] Basing point: White Bird, Idaho. White Bird is in the valley of the Salmon River, 104 mi. south of Lewiston on U. S. Highway 95. The battlefield is at the north edge of town. The unknown soldier's grave is 0.5 mi. north of White Bird on U. S. Highway 95, on the right side of the road. It is well marked.

At the time of the White Bird Battle, Chief Joseph's village was located about where the town of White Bird now stands. The hills in the immediate foreground of the battlefield were the scene of the initial clash, although a running battle was fought all the way to the summit.

"WHEN I am gone think of your country," Old Chief Joseph warned Young Joseph. "Always remember . . . [never] sign a treaty selling your home . . . My son, never forget my dying words."

The beautiful, prolific Wallowa Lake country in eastern Oregon was the ancestral home of the Nez Perce. Although friendly and cooperative with the whites, the Nez Perce were inflexible in their determination to retain this lush land. Only because they were guaranteed the Wallowa and Imnaha valleys did Old Chief Joseph and Chief Looking Glass sign the 1855 treaty offered by Governor Stevens of Washington and General Palmer of Oregon.

But the white men kept encroaching. The Clearwater branch of the Nez Perce finally signed a treaty to go on a reservation at Kamiah. Joseph's tribe whose lands were involved, also was ordered to the reservation although he had not signed the treaty.

Because the 30-day ultimatum to leave the Wallowa country was so short, the Indians lost considerable stock in a river crossing. This, together with the imprisonment of an old chief, Too-hul-hul-sote, stirred resentment among the Nez Perce.

A council was held. Young Chief Joseph argued, "I would give up my country. I would give up my father's grave, I would give up everything rather than have the blood of white men on my people's hands." But the decision was taken from him by three young braves, Walitits, Sarpsus Ilp Pilp and Umtililpcown, who attacked and killed four settlers, Richard Divine, Robert Bland, Henry Elfers and Henry Beckroge.

Other depredations followed. Joseph, who had once said, ". . . Why should the children of one mother and one father quarrel? . . . I do not believe the Great Spirit gave one kind of men the right to tell another kind of men what to do . . ." knew that he would have to lead his people in battle.

General O. O. Howard immediately dispatched Colonel David Perry with 99 Fort Lapwai men from troops F and H, 1st U. S. Cavalry. The officers were Captain Joel G. Trimble and lieutenants William R. Parnell and Edward R. Theller.

VALLEY OF THE SHADOW: White Bird Canyon with the River of No Return (Salmon River Canyon) in the distance.

THE STORM BREAKS: The Nez Perce lay in ambush in the ravine. The troops took up position on the round hill right of center. When the line gave way the retreat that became a mad scramble went over the rocks to the left.

The Nez Perce continued their raids. On June 14, 1877, they killed two settlers and carried off Mrs. John Manuel. John Chamberlain was killed and his wife raped. Their daughter's tongue was removed and their small son murdered by having his skull crushed. These assaults by ever-increasing numbers of the Nez Perce were unauthorized and unattended by Chief Joseph, who was at Salmon River where his wife was in childbirth.

The Indians had disappeared when Perry and his command arrived at the scene. Grangeville citizens told him the Indians had been observed going toward White Bird Canyon on the Salmon River. Colonel Perry feared they might cross the river and escape into the rugged country beyond. Reinforced by 50 volunteers under an ex-Confederate Army officer named Shearer, Perry and his men pressed on in the darkness.

Perry halted his command at the rim of White Bird Canyon. The few remaining hours of night were used to rest. An unnatural coyote call, heard when one of the men lighted his pipe, was scarcely heeded.

"Boots and Saddles" was sounded just before daybreak of June 17, 1877. With the night shadows still in the canyon, Perry's men began the descent. Winding down the steep trail, they made their tortuous way toward the Indian encampment on the canyon floor six miles below. Through field glasses, the officers could see the lodges of the Nez Perce. No activity was apparent, and it seemed a surprise might be possible.

The Nez Perce braves, however, had already crept into their positions. The first battle ever to be fought between the Nez Perce and United States soldiers was about to begin.

The horses slipped and slid as the cavalrymen, with carbines ready, rode down the mountainside. Bullets started flying around Lieutenant Theller and his eight men, who were riding about 100 yards in advance of the main body. They caught fleeting views of the Indians stealing from boulder to boulder.

Lieutenant Theller dismounted his men and deployed them along a ridge. Nine civilians were ordered to hold a knoll at the left of Theller. The volunteers, under Shearer, moved into the high ground left of the civilians. Coming up swiftly, Colonel Perry and Troop F moved in to support Theller. Then a tactical error was made. Trimble, with Troop H, moved up to the right instead of staying on the hill where he could cover a possible retreat. This left no reserves to protect the first line if a retreat were forced by the Indians.

Trumpeter Johnny Jones was the first to fall. Mounted Indians, riding hard and hanging on the sides of their horses, charged the left knoll. Two of the civilian defenders were wounded. The others broke before the furious charge of the red men. "We mixed them up," said Yellow Wolf of this part of the action, "I did some bow shooting. Two of my arrows struck soldiers only five steps away—one in the shoulder—one in the breast. We did not stop to fight the wounded. We chased hard after the others."

The break in the civilian line enabled Chief Joseph and his warriors to open a crossfire on Perry's troops, who were forced to give way to save themselves. Perry lost his trumpet but shouting over the uproar of battle ordered his men to retire to the next ridge. Panic was taking hold among the recruits of Company F.

The mounted Indians charged Trimble's troop, causing it to give also. Seeing everyone retreating, Theller's men were seized by the same panic.

"The whole right of the line," said Perry, later, "seeing the mad rush for horses on the left, also gave way and the panic became general."

The officers beseeched their men to hold together and withdraw fighting. But the fear-ridden men fled in disorder toward the top of the canyon.

Lieutenant Theller and 18 men tried to form a rear guard, but were cut off. "They were in a ravine where grew thorn bushes," recalled Yellow Wolf. "Those soldiers put up a fight . . . [they] were wiped out."

An Irish sergeant lost his horse in the mad flight up the slope. Calling to others as they swarmed past, he asked them at least to leave him cartridges to defend himself. Later his body was found propped against a thorn bush. He was not stripped of clothing or equipment, and sunflowers decorated his hat cord.

The hostiles pursued the fleeing soldiers to the plateau at the top of the canyon. Here the soldiers rallied and began a more disciplined retreat. At last the Indian chiefs commanded, "Let the soldiers go. We have done them enough."

Thirty-three soldiers, nearly a third of those engaged, were killed. Of the some 70 Nez Perce involved, the Indians admitted to three wounded. This may be inaccurate, for the Indians disliked acknowledging their battle losses.

The soldiers' remains were not scalped or mutilated. The only scalp taken in the entire Nez Perce War in northern Idaho was that of an Indian, taken by George M. Shearer, leader of the volunteers.

NO MORE BOOTS AND SADDLES:

The grave of an unknown soldier of Perry's command killed in the White Bird Battle.

THE SEVENTEEN VOLUNTEERS
AT COTTONWOOD

[72] Basing point: Cottonwood, Idaho. Take U. S. Highway 95, 1.4 mi. from the Cottonwood post office, going south. The monument is on the left side of the road.

Troops in the Nez Perce War received supplies from Cottonwood. Many a pioneer journeyed through this little town—a key stage station. Today it retains much of the old western atmosphere.

AFTER THE defeat at White Bird Canyon, Colonel Perry was placed in charge of the supply base at Cottonwood. Indians in great numbers were about. Fearing an overwhelming attack, Perry sent a messenger to Mount Idaho, requesting volunteers as reinforcements.

Captain D. B. Randall with 17 volunteers left Mount Idaho July 5, 1877. Riding hard for about 17 miles, they came within two or three miles of Cottonwood.

On a distant hill they saw a lone Indian horseman silhouetted against the sky. Pausing to watch, they discerned more and more Indians gathering on the hill.

The volunteers were within sight of the soldiers at Cottonwood. As the Indians moved forward, apparently intending to cut off the volunteers, Captain Randall decided on a bold move. He and his 17 men charged right through the Indians.

"Those men made for us," said Yellow Wolf. "We were lined across their path. As they charged we made way . . . then struck after them, racing to flank both sides."

Captain Randall was mortally wounded. He stayed on his horse until it too was shot. The fighting grew close and heavy. It was decided to dismount and fight it out from a knoll.

Ben F. Evans was killed and D. H. Houser wounded. The injured Captain Randall asked Lieutenant Wilmot for water. As Wilmot raised Randall's head to give him a drink, the captain began, "Tell my wife . . ." and died.

Two men were sent to the soldiers at Cottonwood for aid. Perry, perhaps made overly chary by his defeat at White Bird, refused to send assistance.

A Sergeant Simpson could no longer tolerate the sight of the volunteers being massacred in plain sight of the troops. "If your officers won't lead you," Simpson cried, "I will." Twenty-five soldiers joined him, starting for their horses.

Perry, seeing that his men were going with or without the leadership of officers, ordered Major Whipple to lead them. The Indians were driven off and the volunteers brought in.

Two volunteers were killed and three wounded in this action. It is believed at least nine Indians were killed.

Sergeant Simpson was charged with insubordination. The charges were withdrawn after he was seriously wounded in the Clearwater battle.

210

ERECTED IN
MEMORY OF THE
SEVENTEEN VOLUNTEERS
WHO ENGAGED IN BATTLE
WITH THE INDIANS
2000 FEET EAST
FROM THIS POINT
WITH TWO KILLED AND
THREE WOUNDED THE
5TH DAY OF JULY 1877
DURING THE NEZ PERCE INDIAN WAR

CAPTAIN D. B. RANDALL
C. M. DAY, JAMES BUCHANAN, H. C. JOHNSON
F. A. FENN, FRANK D. VANSISE, L. P. WILMOT
A. D. BARTLEY, CHARLES JOHNSON, A. B. LELAND

J. L. CEARLEY, WILLIAM B. BEEMER, D. H. HOWSER
GEORGE RIGGINS

DONATED AND ERECTED BY EVAN EVANS
THROUGH IDAHO COUNTY PIONEER ASSOCIATION
GRANGEVILLE IDAHO
THE 5TH DAY OF JULY 1931

THE RAINS MASSACRE

[73] Basing point: Cottonwood, Idaho. Take U. S. Highway 95 north 0.6 mi. from Cottonwood post office. Turn left on gravel road 0.5 mi. to cemetery. Turn left and continue west. The grave of Scout William Foster is 3.9 mi. from the starting point, on the right side of the road.

The grave of Lieutenant S. M. Rains is in the old Post Cemetery at Walla Walla. (See "The Battle of Clearwater.")

NEWS of hostile Nez Perce Indians in the vicinity came to the U. S. troops stopping at Cottonwood, Idaho, July 3, 1877. Civilian scouts Charles Blewitt, 19, and William Foster, 24, were sent to investigate. They were fired on when they discovered a considerable body of Indians at the head of Lawyers Canyon.

The Indians stated that Blewitt fell, shot through the head. Foster, however, returning to Cottonwood on a lathered horse, reported he did not know what happened to his companion. They had become separated; he had not seen Blewitt since the attack.

On receiving the scout's report Major Whipple, in command of the troops at Cottonwood, took action. He ordered Lieutenant Sevier M. Rains with ten 1st U. S. Cavalrymen to ride toward the Indians and reconnoiter, guided by Foster. Whipple was to follow with the main body.

When Rains' detachment entered a shallow ravine the Indians sprung a trap, pouring bullets on the troopers.

Yellow Wolf, a Nez Perce who participated in the ambush, said later, "I saw about twelve soldiers . . . there was shooting . . . one soldier fell from his horse . . . then another went down . . . I will not hide anything. That part of the fight was not long . . . 6 soldiers did not get up.

"The remaining soldiers ran their horses up the hill, then jumped off among some rocks and began shooting. Those soldiers were trapped . . . their shooting was just like their calling 'Come on, come on, come on,' a calling to death. We crawled toward the soldiers. I will not hide it. Those soldiers were killed."

At first their bodies were buried where they lay. Later they were reinterred in the cemetery at Fort Walla Walla. Lieutenant Rains was buried in a separate grave.

The body of Charles Blewitt was found two and a half months later. He was buried at Cottonwood House, but later was brought to Walla Walla. *The Walla Walla Union Bulletin* described his funeral: "On a September Sunday, the First Cavalry band led the cortege from the Episcopal Church to the cemetery. Members of the garrison followed afoot and each dropped an evergreen on the coffin at the graveside. Volunteers attended and gave thanks to the regulars for their interest."

"COME ON, COME ON"

Upper: The grave of Lieutenant Savier M. Rains in the old cemetery near the Veterans' Hospital at Walla Walla, Washington.

MAN AND HORSE

The grave of Scout William Foster and his horse.

THE SPALDING MISSION

[74] Basing point: Lewiston, Idaho. Take U. S. Highway 95 out Main Street, across Clearwater Bridge. Turn right at end of bridge and go east 11 mi. Here you will find another bridge across the Clearwater. Cross this bridge going south to reach Spalding.

HENRY HARMON SPALDING was a jack-of-all-trades and master of many. Missionary, mechanic, printer, builder, scholar and farmer, he devoted his life to the material and spiritual development of the Indians.

In 1836 Spalding and his wife, Eliza, established a mission on the Clearwater River. To enrich the Indian way of life he taught them soil cultivation along with religion. He established the first printing press in Idaho, the first sawmill, the first gristmill, the first church and the first irrigation project. Eliza started the first Idaho school.

At the time of the Whitman Massacre Spalding was on his way to visit Marcus Whitman, his co-worker at Waiilatpu. A few miles short of his destination he was warned of the uprising by Father Brouillet of the Catholic mission. Fearing for his family, Spalding turned back toward Lapwai. Indians were hunting him, and he narrowly escaped capture on the first night of his return trip. Forcing his horse to lie in tall grass as he held the beast's nose to prevent its calling out to the Indians' horses, he passed that night safely.

The following night he neglected to hobble his horse. It escaped. He continued on foot over the tortuous rock trail, tying his leggings around his feet to replace his too-tight shoes. Arriving at Lapwai, Spalding discovered his fears to be unfounded. The Nez Perce, remaining loyal, had protected his family and mission against the Cayuses.

Because of the unrest following this Indian uprising, the Board of Missions sent Spalding to Oregon. Years later he resumed his work at Lapwai.

The Reverend Spalding died among the people he loved and helped so bountifully, on August 3, 1874. Most of the mourners at the simple funeral services were Nez Perce Indians. He was buried in the cemetery near the mission and church he had built. Spalding left little money. His second wife could not erect his tombstone until three years after his death.

REMAINS OF A MISSION: One of the original buildings of the Spalding Mission.

THE SPALDING MILL: The first gristmill in Idaho stood here.

GROUND SLOWLY BUT FINE: These Spalding millstones are now preserved on the campus of Northern Idaho College of Education.

WHEAT COUNTRY: Spalding's small plot was the first of the many thousands
of acres of rich wheatland that surround Lewiston.

INDIAN JANE SILCOTT

[75] Basing point: Lewiston, Idaho. Take U. S. Highway 95 east on Main Street, across the Clearwater Bridge. Continue north 2.9 mi. up the hill. Turn left on gravel road 0.4 mi. Leave car. Cut across field on left. The grave is not in sight from the road, but can be seen when one walks about a quarter of a mile distance out on the ridge going toward the river.

Lewiston was a turbulent town in the early days as an outfitting spot for the gold fields. River boats, stages and pack trains surged to her, crammed with supplies and gold.

NURSE, guide and helper of the white men, Jane, daughter of Nez Perce Chief Timothy, stepped in where her father feared to tread.

Jane was sixteen when Colonel Steptoe's defeated command entered her father's camp following their battle with the hostile Indians. With the other Indian women she dressed the men's wounds and ministered to their battle injuries.

In 1860 Captain E. D. Pierce and his party of gold seekers asked Chief Timothy to guide them through the Nez Perce country on a prospecting trip. Timothy was friendly, but refused to go. The Indians were beginning to be jealous of their lands, and the chief feared reprisals to his family if he led the party. Jane, then 18, volunteered. Skillfully she guided them over Indian trails to their destination. Wilbur Fiske Bassett discovered gold on this expedition, at what is now known as Pierce City.

Returning to the tent city of Ragtown, now called Lewiston, Jane married a half-breed Nez Perce. Tragedy struck the young woman when her husband died and a son born of the marriage was drowned.

Later she married a Virginian, John Silcott. Eighteen years her senior, he was good to his Indian wife. Jane, noted as an excellent cook and orderly housekeeper, was a congenial mate. Silcott built and operated a ferry across the Clearwater.

Jane was accustomed to the white men's ways but clung to some Indian practices, which eventually caused her death. She could not be persuaded to cover the open fireplace in her home with a grate. One night when she was standing in front of her Indian fireplace, her white woman's clothes caught fire and she burned to death.

Burying her on the hill across the Clearwater overlooking Lewiston, Silcott erected a handsome tombstone over her grave. It is quite a contrast to the pile of rocks marking the spot where he lies buried next to her.

RACE PREJUDICE: The handsome tombstone marks the grave of Indian Jane Silcott. The little rock cairn at the right is the grave of John Silcott, her white husband.

TRENCHES: These fortifications in the park at Lewiston were dug during the Nez Perce War.

LEWIS AND CLARK CAMP IN THE PATAHA VALLEY

[76] Basing point: Pomeroy, Washington. From city limits go east 4.5 mi. on U. S. Highway 410 to Lewis and Clark campsite marker. The camp was on the creek in a grove of cottonwoods to the right.

In the Idaho gold rush days, Pomeroy was a rough and tough stage station. They say it had 20 saloons and gambling places.

ON THEIR RETURN trip, the Lewis and Clark Expedition left the Columbia River at the mouth of the Walla Walla, starting overland via the Walla Walla and Pataha valleys. They headed for the Kooskooskie, now called the Clearwater River, which joins the Snake at Lewiston, Idaho.

The party was guided by a band of Walla Wallas, in reference to whom the Lewis and Clark *Journal* states, "We may indeed justly affirm that of all the Indians whom we have met since leaving the United States, the Wolla Wollahs were the most hospitable, honest and sincere."

During the morning of May 3, 1806, Lewis and Clark were disturbed when their guides turned back abruptly. A little later they were "agreeably surprised by the appearance of Weahkoonut . . . called the Big Horn from the circumstance of his wearing a horn of that animal suspended from his left arm." He had helped guide the party down the Snake River the year before, proving "highly serviceable."

Their *Journal* continues, "We camped for the night in a grove of cottonwoods, after we had had a disagreeable journey of twenty-eight miles . . . we supped very scantily on dried meat and all that was left of our dogs." Clark loathed dog meat, but Lewis and the others learned to prefer it to horse meat or tough elk and venison. Although they staunchly tried to believe that dog meat was a delicacy, on reaching more civilized country they burst into tears of joy at sight of a cow.

On May 4 they ". . . followed the road over the plains north sixty degrees east for four miles to a ravine, where was the source of a small creek, down the rocky sides of which we proceeded to its entrance to Lewis River [The Snake River]."

DOG MEAT WAS A DELICACY: Lewis and Clark camped in this little cotton-wood grove in 1806.

FIRST WALLA WALLA TREATY

[77] Basing point: Walla Walla, Washington. Go to Whitman College Campus, in Walla Walla. Signing of Governor Stevens' treaty with the Indians took place here. There is a marker on the campus dedicated to Chief Lawyer of the Nez Perce. Another marker at Poplar and Alder streets commemorates the signing of the treaty.

"MY PEOPLE, what have you done? You have sold my country." The query of Nez Perce War Chief Looking Glass represented the attitude of many Indians at the 1855 treaty council.

Congress authorized Governor Isaac Stevens of Washington Territory, and General Joel Palmer, Superintendent of Indian Affairs of Oregon Territory, to make treaties with the tribes east of the Cascades, appropriating funds for the purpose. Late in 1854 Stevens sent runners to learn where the Indians wished to meet in council.

Yakima Chief Kamiakin selected an old council ground about where Walla Walla stands. Some 6,000 Indians were called to council, including the Yakima, Nez Perce, Walla Walla and Cayuse. Lieutenant Lawrence Kip, an observer, described their arrival on May 24, 1855:

"We saw them approaching on horseback in one long line. They were almost entirely naked, gaudily painted and decorated with their wild trappings. Their plumes fluttered about them, while below skins and trinkets of all kinds of fantastic embellishments flaunted in the sunshine. Trained from early infancy almost to live on horseback, they sat on their fine animals almost as if they were centaurs. Their horses, too, were arrayed in the most glaring finery . . .

"When about a half mile distant they halted and a half dozen chiefs rode forward and were introduced to Governor Stevens and General Palmer in order of their rank. Then on came the rest of the wild horsemen in single file, clashing their shields, singing and beating their drums as they marched past us. They then formed a circle and dashed around us . . . They would gallop up as if to make a charge, then wheel round and round, sounding their loud whoops . . . then some score or two dismounted and forming a ring danced for about twenty minutes while those surrounding beat time on their drums."

Governor Stevens and General Palmer arrived at the council ground escorted by 47 dragoons under the command of Lieutenant Archibald Gracie.

The commissioners proposed that the Indians sell their lands to the government and go on reservations where the government would maintain schools, mills and

NEAR THIS SITE
MAY 29 TO JUNE 11 1855
WAS HELD THE
GREAT INDIAN COUNCIL
BY GOVERNOR
ISAAC INGALLS STEVENS
WITH CHIEFS OF THE
NEZ PERCE YAKIMA
CAYUSE
AND WALLA WALLA
INDIAN TRIBES
OF WASHINGTON
OREGON AND IDAHO

PLACED HERE BY
NARCISSA PRENTISS CHAPTER DAR
WALLA WALLA

"WHAT HAVE I TO TALK ABOUT?"

blacksmith and carpenter shops. The Nez Perce, under Chief Lawyer, were the only tribesmen who consented. The others assembled daily to hear the speeches. After each speech Young Chief of the Cayuse tribe asked time to think it over. During these intervals he plotted the massacre of the white men and planned an attack on the garrison at The Dalles. Peu-peu-mox-mox of the Walla Wallas and Kamiakin of the Yakimas were co-plotters.

Nez Perce Chief Lawyer forestalled the conspiracy by moving his lodge and family into the white camp to inform the schemers that the whites were under the protection of the powerful Nez Perce.

The council did not go well. "What have I to be talking about?" asked Kamiakin when Stevens appealed to him. Peu-peu-mox-mox wanted to adjourn without a decision, although he and Kamiakin finally agreed to sign. Kamiakin believed the conditions of the treaty might reunite his scattered tribe. He refused the customary present saying, "Don't offer me presents. I have never yet accepted one from a white man. When the government sends the pay for these lands, I will take my share."

The treaties were all signed by June 11, 1855, after three weeks of negotiation. The Nez Perce and Yakimas were to be paid $200,000 each. The Cayuse, Walla Walla and Umatilla tribes, who were to be located together, were to receive $150,000.

Kamiakin, Peu-peu-mox-mox and their tribes subsequently violated the treaties Years later when Kamiakin was offered "his share" he said that although he was very poor he was still too rich to accept anything from the United States Government.

FREED: As Indian resistance was broken in the wars that followed the treaty, many of the Indian leaders were taken prisoner. Twenty-four were executed after Colonel Wright's campaign. This may have been one of them.

KNOWN BUT TO GOD: The grave of a soldier, trader, trapper, Indian or pioneer in the Fort Walla Walla cemetery.

THE BATTLE OF CLEARWATER

[78] Basing point: Walla Walla, Washington. Go west on Main Street. On reaching Twelfth Avenue, one block from the Union Pacific Depot, turn left and go 5 blocks to West Chestnut. Turn right through entrance to Veterans' Hospital. Follow road through hospital grounds to the chapel. Take gravel road left of chapel across an alfalfa field to the cemetery. The cemetery is 1.2 mi. from the hospital entrance.

Walla Walla was council ground for the Indian tribes during many decades. The name means "many waters." Main Street follows almost exactly an old Indian warpath.

Because the dead from the battle of Clearwater are buried in the Walla Walla cemetery, the story of the battle is given here. The Clearwater Battlefield is not easily accessible on this tour.

ON THE MORNING of July 11, 1877, only a little more than a week after the Rains' massacre, General O. O. Howard ordered his command to proceed to the Clearwater River. Troop E, 1st U. S. Cavalry, under Captain Winter led the column. Following were troops F, L and H, four companies of infantry and four artillery companies—about 400 men in all. Indians were encountered at the mouth of Cottonwood Creek on the Clearwater River in Idaho.

Nez Perce Chief Joseph, often called the Red Napoleon because of his great ability as a military strategist, had carefully chosen the place. The Indians were well-armed and well-entrenched.

The battle commenced at noon. In the bitter but inconclusive fighting through the afternoon, Howard's troops were cut off from the water supply. The Indians hurled taunting insults at the soldiers. Inspired by Joseph they sometimes charged to the troops' bayonet points. Desperate for water, the soldiers counterattacked, successfully, but the Indian snipers still commanded the spring. It looked as if Howard, who had been one of the Northern strategists at Gettysburg, had met his master.

Without water or the dangerous comfort of campfires, the troops spent a wretched night. From the Indian camp in the river bottom they could hear the moan of the death song and the scalp chant. Occasionally the voices of chiefs Joseph, Ollicut and White Bird could be distinguished inspiring the braves to greater deeds the following day.

At dawn the troops swiftly charged the Indian barricades around the spring, securing the water supply. After the thirsty soldiers filled their canteens and had a meager breakfast, they renewed the attack. In the afternoon a pack train with needed supplies accompanied by a cavalry troop arrived. As the fighting increased in intensity, effective maneuvering gave the soldiers the advantage. General Howard ordered a full charge of all troops to press the advantage.

The Indians fled wildly across the river. Joseph restored order among them and

226

they withdrew toward Kamiah. During the battle both General Howard and Chief Joseph showed exceptional disregard for their own safety. This bravery gave the two enemy leaders a mutual respect for each other.

The next day burial parties interred 13 soldiers and 15 warriors. Eight more Indian bodies were found on the trail later. Twenty-four soldiers were wounded, according to General Howard's report. Yellow Wolf stated positively that only four Indians were killed.

The slain were at first buried where they fell. Later they were taken to Walla Walla. This accounts for the difficulty in identifying them, and the common grave.

IN HONORED GLORY: The common grave of the 13 soldiers who fell in the Battle of Clearwater.

WHITMAN MASSACRE
AT WAIILATPU

[79] Basing point: Walla Walla, Washington. From the Northern Pacific Railroad Depot, go 5.1 mi. west on U. S. Highway 410. Here there is a sign with directions to Waiilatpu. Turn left on gravel road 1 mi. to the monument, which can be seen on hill to right. The common grave of the Whitman massacre victims is at the foot of the hill. Site of the mission was to the right of the road where a grove of poplars now stands.

Traces of the old mill pond are still clearly visible. The National Park Service is excavating the ruins of the mission and maintains a museum on the grounds. The present road to Waiilatpu follows the Old Oregon Trail.

HAVING HEARD the story of Jesus through fur traders, the Nez Perce sent four braves on foot the 2,000 miles to St. Louis and back to inquire about the new religion.

When their story was publicized the American Board of Missions sent missionaries to satisfy the Indians' spiritual hunger. Dr. Marcus Whitman was the most notable of these. After a long, bitterly-difficult trip overland he arrived with his wife, Narcissa, at Waiilatpu, near Walla Walla. There he built his mission in 1836.

Although primarily a medical missionary, Dr. Whitman taught Christianity to his interested charges. The Indians grew to love and respect the doctor and his wife. Whitman, with his boundless strength and energy, gave them schooling and taught them farming as well as treating them medically. Charming Narcissa Whitman was gentle, helpful and kind to all who came to the mission.

In 1847 the attitude of mutual confidence between the Whitmans and the Indians began to change subtly. Told that Dr. Whitman was giving them poison instead of medicine in order to gain their lands, the Cayuse Indians under Chief Tilaukait became suspicious. An outbreak of measles killed many of the Indians, furthering their belief that the doctor was destroying them.

During the fall of 1847 Whitman was conscious of imminent disaster. His letters to friends in the East showed his dread. Conversation around the mission became guarded. He was heard to say, "If things do not clear up I will have to leave in the spring."

On November 28 the doctor, who had been to Umatilla, stopped at the lodge of Stickas, an Indian friend. His sense of foreboding increased as he heard the Indians chanting the death song. As he hurried homeward an Indian woman warned him not to go to Waiilatpu. This only served to make him go faster. Everything he loved was at the "Place of Rye Grass."

Whitman confided his fears to Narcissa that night. In the morning it was observed Mrs. Whitman had been crying and ate no breakfast. The doctor went about the affairs of the mission as usual, but said to his wife, "Why do you suppose so many

THERE WAS ALWAYS THUNDER IN THE OFFING: The Whitman monument. Trouble was impending almost from the day the Whitmans arrived at Waiilatpu.

Indians are gathered round today?" although a beef was being butchered, which always attracted numbers of them. Their weapons were kept concealed beneath their blankets.

Chiefs Tilaukait and Tamsuky knocked at the mission door demanding medicine. Dr. Whitman admitted them into the kitchen. While Tilaukait engaged the doctor in conversation, Tamsuky drew a pipe tomahawk from under his blanket and twice smashed it in Whitman's skull. John Sager, just entering the kitchen, was shot dead. Jim Bridger's daughter, whom the Whitmans had adopted, escaped around the house and ran to Mrs. Whitman, crying, "They have killed father!"

Narcissa Whitman remained calm, but clasped her hands on hearing more shots, and said, "The Indians will murder us all." There was no outcry and no tears. With two other women she went to the doctor; they carried him to the dining room. Whitman was still living, but could only whisper, "No," when his wife asked if she could do anything for him. She broke a little then, and exclaimed, "I am a widow, I am a widow!" But she eased a pillow under the doctor's head and tried to stop the flow of blood.

Outside, Mr. Saunders, the school teacher, was set upon by three Indians. One grappled with him, another sought a chance to plunge his knife into him, and the third stood by with a gun. Although Saunders broke away and ran for the mission house, he was shot as he attempted to scramble over a fence.

Through a window Mrs. Whitman was shot under the left arm. Near the scene of the beef dressing, Jacob Hoffman and a man named Marsh were killed. Isaac Gillen was shot sitting at a table in the emigrant house.

Craftily, Tamsuky offered to guide the survivors in the mission house to the emigrant house, saying the former was about to be burned. As they stepped out Tamsuky darted away from the range of fire. Mrs. Whitman was shot again. A Mr. Rogers, who had previously been wounded, was killed. Francis Sager was singled out from the children and killed. The rest of the women and children were conducted safely to the emigrant house.

Narcissa Whitman, dying in the schoolhouse where she had been carried, expressed concern for the many children they had adopted, who would now be orphaned again. Knowing she had but a few minutes to live, she prayed for their welfare.

Crockett Bewley and Amos Sales, lying ill at the mission house, were not molested at first. Perhaps the Indians thought they would die soon, anyway. After a few days when they appeared to be getting better the Indians clubbed them to death.

Several men escaped the massacre by hiding in the emigrant house and other places until nightfall and then slipping away. Among them was Peter Hall, who left his wife and five children at the mission and fled to Fort Walla Walla. Arriving there completely demented, he stole an Indian canoe and disappeared down the Columbia. He was never heard of again.

The Osborne family of five escaped at night. Mrs. Osborne was an invalid. Os-

PLACE OF RYE GRASS: The site of the mission house at Waiilatpu. The sign marks the front door where Mrs. Whitman daily left on her pilgrimage to the grave of her little girl who drowned in the Walla Walla River.

EMIGRANT HOUSE: Built to take care of visitors from the Oregon Trail, this was the house where the Whitman survivors were held by the Indians.

borne concealed her and two older children, then carried his two-year-old boy on his back to Fort Walla Walla. He was given horses at the fort and returned to bring the rest of his family to safety.

The Indians held for ransom the 46 survivors, mostly women and children. The prisoners were treated well, for the most part. Peter Skene Ogden of the Hudson's Bay Company arranged for their release. In ransom he paid 62 blankets, 63 shirts, 600 rounds of ammunition, 37 pounds of tobacco and 12 flints.

The mission had been burned. Reverend Brouillet of the Catholic mission buried the bodies of the slain.

A nephew of the doctor, Perrine Whitman, visited the site of the mission in April, 1848. "We found everything swept from the site of the Mission," he reported in the *Whitman College Quarterly* for 1898, "the buildings burned and everything in ruins. The bodies had been buried, but coyotes had dug into the graves considerable. I found what I satisfied myself was the Doctor's skull. There were two hatchet marks in the back of the head."

The remains were gathered and buried in a common grave covered by a wagon box.

THE WHITMAN TOMB

THE FIRST HOME: Whitman and his wife lived here until the larger mission house was finished.

SITE OF THE GRISTMILL: The outlines of the old dam and the mill pond still can be seen clearly.

BATTLE OF FRENCHTOWN

[80] Basing point: Walla Walla, Washington. Take Highway 410 west 6.2 mi. to monument marking the site of Frenchtown. From this point on the hill the monument marking the location of the Old St. Rose Mission Cemetery can be seen clearly 0.25 mi. to the north. There is no road, but it can be reached by walking across the intervening field.

As GOVERNOR STEVENS was tying the final loose strings in the series of Indian treaties, the earlier agreements were fast unraveling.

The governor was concluding his treaty with the Blackfeet at Fort Benton when a messenger warned him of serious outbreaks among the Yakimas, Cayuses and Walla Wallas. Bitterness over the harsh impositions of the treaties intensified the Indians' anxiety to retain their lands. The tribes were murdering settlers in the Puget Sound country and in the country of the Yakimas.

Chief Peu-peu-mox-mox, or Yellow Nose, of the Walla Wallas had threatened to kill Stevens as he returned. Lieutenant Colonel James K. Kelley with six companies of Oregon Volunteers was dispatched to meet the governor to protect him from assassination.

When Kelley arrived at Fort Walla Walla he found it had been pillaged by the Indians and was deserted. He led his troops in pursuit of the warriors up the Touchet River.

Peu-peu-mox-mox, with an entourage of warriors, on December 6, 1855, brought a flag of truce into Kelley's camp. The lieutenant regarded this gesture of peace with a grain of salt, for the chief was surly and his actions belied the goodwill the flag was supposed to convey. Kelley felt he was stalling for time so his tribe could escape. Warily, Kelley detained the chief and six of his followers, thereby violating the flag of truce.

Moving on toward Waiilatpu, Kelley and his men faced gunfire from Indians hidden in the brush along the river. Forced to stop, the troops had a chilling preview of what lay ahead. Shouting Indians pounded their horses over the surrounding hills, riding swiftly alone or in groups. More and more appeared. Poles bearing the limp, pathetic scalps of white settlers were the center of dancing, battle-hungry tribesmen. The battle began around a little covey of pioneers' houses called Frenchtown.

The Indians barricaded themselves in one of the houses, but howitzer fire by the troops dislodged them. That first day several soldiers were killed. As the conflict increased in intensity the excited Peu-peu-mox-mox yelled encouragement to his warriors. Shouting orders, and growing more frenzied by the minute, he at last tried to snatch a gun from a guard. This thoughtless over-confidence was fatal. He was instantly killed by a blow on the head. The soldiers scalped him and cut off his ears.

HERE STOOD
ST. ROSE MISSION
ALSO KNOWN AS
FRENCHTOWN
1850 ←——→ 1900
LAND DONATION CLAIM
OF NARCISSE REYMOND
CEMETERY ON HILL NORTH
OREGON VOLUNTEERS FOUGHT
INDIANS DEC. 7, 8, 9, 1855
CHIEF PEU-PEU-MOX-MOX
OF WALLA WALLA'S SLAIN.

Erected by home economic
clubs of Walla Walla Co.

During the cold night of December 7, the troops hurriedly extinguished their campfires, before which they made good targets. Next morning the Indians closed in again. More braves had joined the fight. And so the battle see-sawed. By December 10 the Indians seemed to have the advantage. They had thrown up breastworks, and their ranks still increased. The situation was desperate for the troops until a cavalry charge drove the hostiles from their fortification. The Indians scattered and did not return. The troops continued on their mission to meet Governor Stevens at Waiilatpu.

The ears of Peu-peu-mox-mox were preserved in whiskey. One night the liquor disappeared. For some time the rather ghoulish question went the rounds, "Who drank the whiskey off Peu-peu-mox-mox's ears?" The ears were sent to Salem where for some time they were nailed up on the state house.

SIGN OF THE CROSS: The monument marking the old cemetery at French-town.

FORT NEZ PERCE

[81] Basing point: Wallula, Washington: Wallula is on U. S. Highway 410, 29 mi. west of Walla Walla. Turn west off the main road at the gas station at the east end of the bridge over the Walla Walla River. Go 0.3 mi. to an old abandoned building labeled Hotel Wallula. Turn left across the railroad tracks. Follow paved road 0.25 mi. to school. Turn left again on gravel road 1.15 mi. to where the main road turns sharply right. Take unimproved road straight ahead through sagebrush. This is probably the same road traveled 100 years ago by pioneers and apparently has not been improved or repaired since, but it is usable. Continue 1 mi. to where some boathouses stand on the banks of the Columbia. At the monument, the outline of the walls of the fort still show clearly.

The Lewis and Clark Expedition made the first recorded visit of white men to this region. On their way to the Pacific in the fall of 1805 they camped at the confluence of the Snake and Columbia rivers, a mile or two above the site of Fort Walla Walla. They passed this very place in their dugouts on their way down the river. Returning from the Pacific Coast they went to the mouth of the Walla Walla, half a mile below the site of the fort, from where they proceeded eastward on land. Their *Journal* remarks that in this vicinity they killed several rattlesnakes which were "like those of the United States."

Wallula, now a little sagebrush-surrounded railroad town, was a lively place in pioneer days. It was the connecting point between stage lines running to the Idaho gold fields and the Columbia River boats. Its Indian name means essentially the same as Walla Walla: many waters.

THE BRITISH were way ahead of the Americans in the fur game. Trappers of the Hudson's Bay Company and their Canadian competitor, the North West Company, were eyeing the Pacific Northwest hoping to expand their conquest of the fur trade.

When Lewis and Clark reported on the region, American commercial companies decided to challenge the British monopoly by getting there first. John Jacob Astor sent two expeditions to the Oregon country in 1810, one by land and one by sea. The sea party reached the mouth of the Columbia River, founding a trading post at Astoria on April 12, 1811. After extreme hardship the land expedition crossed the mountains, probably reaching the Columbia at its conjunction with the Walla Walla. During January, 1812, they floated down the Columbia to straggle into Astoria.

When everything seemed to conspire to make Astor's enterprises fail, he sold out to the North West Company. The first man to realize the possibilities of a post where the Walla Walla meets the Columbia was huge, competent Donald McKenzie of the North West Company. He and 95 others started building Fort Nez Perce in July, 1818.

Because timber was scarce, logs were floated down the river. The men constructed a palisade 20 feet high of heavy timber around the 200-foot-square enclosure. Two bastions at diagonal corners and water tanks of 200 gallon capacity afforded

238

WAGON WHEEL EROSION: Along the approach to Fort Nez Perce the ruts are nearly four feet deep in places. This perhaps is the only remaining remnant of the Oregon Trail still in use and still unimproved.

TO DUST RETURNED: The rock foundations of the walls of Fort Nez Perce. One of the bastions stood about where the concrete block lies at right center.

greater protection from possible Indian attacks. Inside the walls were several drift-wood houses and one of stone.

McKenzie and those who followed him found the fort profitable. It was the one small spot of civilization in the tremendous area between St. Louis and the Pacific.

Eventually the Hudson's Bay Company bought the fort. Pierre Pambrun, a veteran of the War of 1812, became a noted factor because of his courtesy and hospitality to those who visited or traded here. Only Americans seeking supplies for fur-trading excursions were rebuffed. Pambrun, like other Hudson's Bay factors, was not going to allow the reins to slip into American hands.

Various kinds of diplomacy were necessary to run a fort. When Archibald McKinley was factor, an inexperienced clerk struck an Indian boy during an argument over some birchwood. Peu-peu-mox-mox and 50 warriors angrily strode to the fort to avenge the insult. Exhibiting a keg of gunpowder, McKinley stood over it with flint and steel. As he threatened to strike the powder the braves gave up their ideas of vengeance. They fled while their chief backed out after them.

When the wooden fort burned down in 1842 it was rebuilt of adobe.

The Indian wars of 1855 meant the end of trade at the fort. The Yakimas and Walla Wallas were openly rebellious. Settlers faced warfare. The Dalles Indian agent Nathan Olney notified the three Hudson's Bay officers at Fort Nez Perce of the uprising. Disposing of much of their ammunition in the Columbia River, the officers left the rest of the stores with a friendly Walla Walla chief at the fort. The powerful Peu-peu-mox-mox and his tribesmen overwhelmed the friendly chief and plundered the fort.

When Lieutenant Colonel James Kelley and his Oregon Volunteers stopped here during a campaign into the Yakima country, they found the fort deserted. The abandoned fort stood as a landmark until partly washed away by the 1894 flood of the Columbia River.

WALLULA GAP: View up the Columbia toward Fort Nez Perce. The monument-shaped rock and its mate just back of it are called The Twin Sisters.

THE MIGHTY OREGON: The pageant of history flowed down the Columbia River.

SACAJAWEA

[82] Basing point: Pasco, Washington. From city limits go 2.3 mi. east on U. S. Highway 410. There you will find large highway department sign pertaining to Sacajawea. Turn right over 2.2 mi. of good road to Sacajawea Park, at the junction of the Snake and Columbia rivers.

Pasco went from rags to riches during World War II. The nearby Hanford atomic bomb project and Naval Air Force base meant many new buildings and a great population increase for the once unprepossessing town.

The beautiful Sacajawea Park was the campsite of Lewis and Clark and their party on their trip to the Pacific Ocean.

IF SACAJAWEA had not been kidnapped, she might have remained unknown.

A Shoshone, she was born in approximately 1786. As she grew up among her tribe near the headwaters of the Salmon River in Idaho, her life was that of any young Indian woman. Her name means the Bird Woman or the Boat Paddler. There is no way of knowing which is correct. It could be either.

The Shoshones habitually made expeditions into buffalo country for meat and winter robes. The Blackfeet Indians attacked the party on one of these trips. Sacajawea was taken prisoner. Later she was traded or given as a slave to the Minatarees.

Toussaint Charbonneau, a Frenchman employed by the North West Fur Company, purchased her from the Minataree tribe for a wife.

When Lewis and Clark wintered in North Dakota, they engaged Charbonneau to accompany their expedition. Their *Journal* entry of April 7, 1805, reads, "The wife of Charbonneau accompanied us with her small child and we hope may be useful as an interpreter among the Snake Indians."

By the time Lewis and Clark had reached the Continental Divide, they realized that Sacajawea was of much greater value to them than was her abusive husband.

Immediately after crossing the Divide they encountered a band of Shoshone Indians whose chief, Cameahwait, was the brother of Sacajawea. Friendly relations with the tribesmen, plus Sacajawea's knowledge of the country of her girlhood, aided the expedition immeasurably. She made the entire trip to the Pacific and return.

"With her helpless infant she rode with the men, guiding us unerringly through mountain passes and lonely places," the *Journal* reads. "Intelligent, cheerful, resourceful, tireless, faithful, she inspired us all."

Sacajawea and Charbonneau separated after the expedition. In her wandering life she married a Comanche Indian with whom she lived many years until his death. Later she married a Frenchman who was killed shortly after.

Her son, Baptiste, took her to the Shoshone Agency in 1871 requesting care for his old mother. She died at the Shoshone Reservation in 1884.

WIDE WATERS

The junction of the Snake and Columbia rivers.

THE BIRD WOMAN

Statue of Sacajawea.

FORT SIMCOE

[83] Basing point: Toppenish, Washington. Take State Highway 3B from Toppenish straight west through the Yakima Indian Reservation 20 mi. to White Swan. Continue west about 3 mi., then south 5 mi. to Fort Simcoe.

The atmosphere of the old West prevails in Toppenish. Moccasin-shod Indians, wearing bright shawls and shirts, roam the streets.

Skloom, the brother of Chief Kamiakin, is buried in the Indian cemetery on Toppenish Creek.

In the cemetery at Simcoe is the grave of Lieutenant Jesse K. Allen, who was shot accidentally by his own men during a surprise attack on a hostile Indian village during Major Garnett's campaign.

THE SITE of Fort Simcoe was an ancient council ground for the Indians. They called it "Mool-mool," or Bubbling Water, because of a cold spring there.

George B. McClellan visited the locale as a young lieutenant in 1853. He reported the Yakima Indians had had a fort there as early as 1849 for use in defense against their Cayuse enemies.

In the early summer of 1855, prospectors J. C. Avery, Eugene Barrier, Charles Walker, L. O. Merilet and a man named Jamieson were ambushed near Simcoe. The party had been heading for Colville.

Jamieson and Walker, in the lead, were shot by Indians. The others escaped by concealing themselves. Hiding by day and traveling under cover of night, they carried the news to Seattle. This event, coupled with the murder of an Indian agent named Bolon, signaled the beginning of the Indian Wars of 1855–56. Two of the three Bolon murderers, Stohan and Wappichoh, were brought to Fort Simcoe and hanged.

Colonel George Wright selected the location as logical for a fort in August, 1856. Major Robert S. Garnett, who became a Confederate general and was killed in '61, directed the building of the post. It was originally a crude affair, built of materials secured in the vicinity. Later a more elaborate post was erected. Four of the buildings were constructed in Maine, knocked down and shipped around Cape Horn to the Columbia River. From there, pack trains carried them over the hills to Fort Simcoe.

The fort was abandoned by the military in 1859 and turned over to the Indian Department.

The first two Indian agents appointed by President Lincoln were guilty of graft and mishandling of the Indians. Lincoln subsequently assigned James H. Wilbur to the position in 1864. Known to the Indians as Father Wilbur, he held office for 16 years. Fair and honest, he was also severe. It was said an oak tree near one of the buildings served as a whipping post.

SILENT SENTINEL: The only remaining blockhouse at Fort Simcoe.

PARADE REST: The grounds at Fort Simcoe where troops paraded nearly a century ago is now a wheatfield.

BATTLE OF PAHOTICUTE

[84] Basing point: Yakima, Washington. Take U. S. Highway 410, 5.3 mi. east to Union Gap. Go 0.1 mi. east to viaduct. Cross viaduct, continue 1.3 mi. to monument.

MAJOR GABRIEL J. RAINS led about 700 regulars and volunteers into the Yakima country October 30, 1855. They were accompanied by Colonel J. W. Nesmith of the Oregon Volunteers and Lieutenant Phil H. Sheridan. November 9 they contacted the Yakimas at Union Gap, called by the Indians Pahoticute: Mountain Heads Coming Together.

The Indians were fortified behind stone breastworks which soon were scattered by mortar fire.

Major Rains proceeded with too much caution to suit the Oregon Volunteers. Sheridan, later to become the famous Civil War cavalry general, wrote in his *Personal Memoirs* ". . . our commanding officer decided that it was best to go into camp . . . I proposed that he let me charge with my dragoons . . . his extreme caution led him to refuse the suggestion . . ."

The Indians made plain their contempt of the soldiers, who waited restlessly for orders to charge. "In addition to firing occasionally," wrote Sheridan, "they called us all sorts of bad names, made indecent gestures and aggravated us, so that between 3 and 4 o'clock in the afternoon, by an inexplicable concert of action, and with a serious breach of discipline, a large number of the men and . . . officers broke *en masse* from the camp with loud yells and charged the offending savages."

Although the troops drove the Indians off the hill with no casualties on either side, Rains ordered his men back to camp. Before leaving the hill the men built a bonfire of celebration. When the soldiers went back to camp, Sheridan said, ". . . the Indians returned . . . seemingly to enjoy the fire that had been so generously built for their benefit . . ."

Next day the Indians still held the hill but were routed by the troops.

One old Indian riding a lame horse could not keep up with his fleeing tribesmen. Cut-Mouth-John, Rains' Indian guide, pursued and killed the almost helpless fugitive. The white troops, according to Sheridan, expressed deep scorn for Cut-Mouth-John's action, particularly when he proudly paraded on horseback flourishing his victim's scalp from his bridle.

246

YAKIMA WAR
BATTLE OF
PAHOTICUTE — TWO BUTTES
Nov. 9, 1855
ERECTED BY D.A.R.
JULY 4, 1916

IN MEMORY OF
TOW-TOW-NAH-HEE
A NON COMBATENT KILLED
3-1/2 MILES NORTH OF HERE
BY OW-HAH-TAH-MA-SO
A GOV'T. SCOUT.
YAKIMA WAR 1855-56.
THE ONLY INDIAN HURT IN
THE BATTLE OF
PAH-OY-TI-KOOT.
ERECTED BY THE YAKIMAS AND
FRIENDS   NOV. 9, 1917

**DIFFERENCE OF
OPINION**

Side by side but miles apart
in their spelling, these two
monuments disagree as do
most authorities on the pho-
netic spelling of Indian
names.

EARLY ST. LOUIS AND MANUEL LISA

[85] Basing point: St. Louis, Mo. To reach old St. Louis, go to the Jefferson National Expansion Memorial. It is at the eastern edge of the main business district. Go straight east on Market St. to the Memorial Center. Manuel Lisa's rock house is here, and old cobblestone streets, and markers pointing out the sites of historic homes and buildings. Here, also, is the Old Cathedral, built on the site of the first church in St. Louis in 1764, and the old courthouse which has a fine museum. At the corner of Walnut and Main, Meriwether Lewis participated in the Louisiana Purchase ceremony which gave the United States 1,172,000 square miles of territory.

FUR TRADERS and adventurers often outfitted themselves at LaClede's Village before setting off into the unknown western wilderness. This little settlement, just south of the junction of the Missouri and Mississippi, was actually named St. Louis, after Louis XV. But the villagers preferred to call it by one of its founders' names. Pierre LaClede Liguest and Gilbert de St. Maxent had been French merchants in New Orleans, licensed by the French Governor to stir up trade among the Indians. This was the place they had chosen for a post, and on February 14, 1764, a crew headed by August Chouteau started building.

The post was in a strategic position and it wasn't long before people started pouring in. LaClede's Village, according to Washington Irving, soon ". . . possessed a motley population comprised of the Creole descendants of the original French colonists; the keen traders from the Atlantic States; the backwoodsmen of Kentucky and Tennessee; the Indians and halfbreeds of the prairies; together with a singular aquatic race that had grown up from navigation of the rivers—the boatmen of the Mississippi; who possessed habits, manners, and almost a language peculiarly their own."

Intermarriage was common partly because of the scarcity of white women and partly because the French, mainly interested in fur trade, wanted close understanding with the Indians. Consequently, much of the population were "mongrel Indians and mongrel Frenchmen."

Manuel Lisa was a bold and enterprising Spaniard who had a number of interests in St. Louis as well as more far-flung trading posts. When Wilson Price Hunt was trying to recruit a party in St. Louis for Astor's overland expedition in the early 1800's, he found Lisa a wily competitor. Lisa was trying to assemble a crew, also, to go to his trading post far up the Missouri. He bid high for the services of good men. The two men started vying for Pierre Dorion, the experienced half-breed guide. Dorion had hung around Lisa's establishment enough to build up quite a whiskey bill. To force the guide to accompany him, Lisa threatened to collect the debt. Dorion used the pressure to drive a bargain with Hunt and ended up, not only going with Hunt, but taking along his Indian wife and children.

MANUEL LISA'S ROCK HOUSE: Built in 1810. The man sleeping on the porch is no relation to Pierre Dorion.

ST. CHARLES: Civilization's last outpost on the Missouri during the days of Lewis and Clark and the early fur traders. This town still reflects the French influence of its founders.

Although this gave the Wilson Price Hunt party a head start, Lisa was still thinking up ways to snare Dorion. He hoped to have him served with a writ when the party went through St. Charles. But Dorion had heard of the plan and disappeared into the tall timber until it was safe to show his face again.

Lisa was not too daunted by lack of the guide. He had a superior crew and he knew this stretch of the river like a book. His party sped on. In two months, covering 1,100 miles, Lisa finally caught up with his competitor.

Now it was time to try for Dorion again. Lisa got him aboard his boat, gave him plenty to drink and tried to lure him into deserting Hunt. After he'd had all the whiskey he cared for, Dorion pointed out that Lisa had nothing more to offer. Lisa reminded him of the old debt, and the guide stalked drunkenly from the boat.

He went to Hunt's tent, and was telling him of his competitor's perfidy when Lisa came in. Dorion struck him and, in Washington Irving's words, "a scene of uproar and hubbub ensued that defies description." Knives flashed as Lisa and the guide fought. Others remembered old grudges and grabbed their guns. When Hunt tried to stop the melee, Lisa cursed him bitterly. Hunt immediately forsook his role of mediator for that of participant and challenged Lisa to a personal duel. The angry Spaniard rushed back to his boat for his gun. There, two men of his party restrained him and the fight was over.

Next day the two parties moved on up the river on opposite sides, eyeing each other jealously, "and all personal intercourse ceased between them."

FORT LARAMIE

[86] Basing point: Fort Laramie, Wyoming. From the center of town take marked dirt road to the left, across the military bridge on the North Platte River, 2 mi. to the Fort Laramie National Monument. The bridge, built in 1876, is thought to be the oldest bridge still in use west of the Missouri.

THE INTERSECTION of the great trail to the Oregon country in the west and the trappers' trail which led south to Taos was strategically important early in the 1800's, and down through that century.

As more and more trappers and fur traders gathered here, William Sublette and Robert Campbell were inspired to found a trading post in 1834. The next year they sold Fort William, as it was called, to James Bridger and Thomas Kirkpatrick, who in turn sold it to the American Fur Company.

The post did a booming business. Here was not only a place for fur men to get supplies and dicker with buyers, but a spot where they could go to break the lonely vigils on the trapping lines.

When the first hardy immigrants to the West were increased by thousands, the isolated fur post became a way point on the Oregon Trail. At the fort, which the American Fur Company had renamed Fort John, pioneers repaired their wagons, strengthened their livestock on the tall grass that covered the surrounding hills, rearranged their loads and abandoned unnecessary material. Here the sick were given time to get well or die. Rufus Sage in his book *Rocky Mountain Life* tells of the many who were buried with only "the winds and the wolves to howl their requiem."

The Indians watched the ever-increasing influx of whites with fear for their lands—fear which at times led to violence. Apparently the American Fur Company was not too good as a protector of immigrants, judging by Sage's story of a factor who refused to trade a plug of tobacco for a white captive of the Indians. In 1849 the government bought the fort and changed the name to Laramie, in honor of a French Canadian trapper, Jacques Laramé, who was killed by Indians on the banks of the river now called Laramie. They set up a military post.

The stream of covered wagons continued to flow, and Fort Laramie was an important point of the pony express until the Union Pacific was completed. Although the military garrison dwindled during the Civil War, it was increased later when Red Cloud and his Sioux warriors grew more uneasy about the arrival of the railroads. The government built other posts on the Bozeman Road to the Montana gold fields. Fort Phil Kearny, 230 miles to the north, was among them.

Although a bitter storm raged on Christmas Eve of 1866, Old Bedlam, the officers' quarters at Laramie, was a gay place. Wives in unfamiliar party dresses and

FORT LARAMIE: Famous military post on the Oregon Trail. Most of the buildings are well-preserved or well-repaired. This one, the army hospital, is in ruins.

OLD BEDLAM: Officers' quarters at Fort Laramie.

officers in best blues were having a dance. Outside, walking his post in the storm, the sentry challenged a lone horseman. It was John Philips, a veteran scout, riding a horse which was so exhausted it dropped dead when he arrived.

Wearily Philips told his terrible news. Captain Fetterman and a party of 80 men had been ambushed while out getting wood near Fort Phil Kearny. The Indians had massacred them to the last man. The celebration at Old Bedlam ceased as officers called their companies to arms. Soon they were off to relieve the besieged men at Fort Phil Kearny.

There were a few years of peace after Red Cloud signed a treaty in 1867. Then gold was discovered in the Black Hills. The Sioux again went on the warpath as gold-crazed whites poured in. More soldiers were ordered to the fort, which became a base for operations against Sitting Bull, Crazy Horse and the Sioux who defeated Custer on the Little Bighorn.

By 1878 the Sioux were filtering back to their reservation. Immigrants were settling in Wyoming and the era of the great cattle ranches began. The need for soldiers at Fort Laramie grew less and less. Finally, in 1899, the last of the blue-coated cavalry rode eastward over the bridge of the North Platte.

OLD TIMER: Built by U.S. Army engineers, used by cavalrymen and Indian fighters, covered wagons and cattlemen, it is still in the service.

THE RETIRED TRAVELER: Wagons of this type carried thousands westward.

CHIMNEY ROCK: One of the most distinctive landmarks on the Oregon Trail. This rock was almost always mentioned in the diaries of early travelers.

HALFWAY WEST: Independence Rock marked the halfway point for the westward-bound pioneers. The names and dates they scratched on the rock still show. Much farther west than Fort Laramie, it was equally important to the pioneers.

THE DEATH OF SERGEANT FLOYD

[87] Basing point: Sioux City, Iowa. Drive south along main highway to city limits. Turn right, about 100 yards.

Floyd was buried on a bluff which kept crumbling away until his bones were exposed. Citizens of Sioux City lowered themselves on ropes to rescue his remains and bury them on higher ground. This monument also commemorates the Louisiana Purchase.

Although drilled rigorously by Capt. Clark and Sergeant Ordway through the winter of 1803 and '04, the men of the Lewis and Clark expedition were just getting into condition for their long trek to the Pacific Ocean when they moved up the Missouri in the summer heat. Boils and dysentery plagued them and morale was low. "I am verry sick and has ben for some time," Sergeant Charles Floyd wrote in his diary.

Lewis and Clark diagnosed his illness as "bilious colic." Alarmed when Floyd grew steadily worse in spite of all that they with their limited medical knowledge could do, the captains and men attended him unceasingly.

August 20 Floyd lay in the boat as the expedition moved on up the river under a gentle breeze. His pulse grew steadily fainter and he vomited weakly. The captains, realizing the end was near, had the boat pulled ashore to a sandbar. Floyd whispered, "I am going away." A moment later Sergeant Charles Floyd, a soldier of the United States, died.

His comrades carried Floyd's body across the river and to the top of a bluff overlooking the Missouri. He was buried with the honors of war, and "much lamented," according to Clark's journal. The men erected a cedar post over his grave, inscribed "Sergt. C. Floyd died here 20th of August 1804." That night the party made camp at the mouth of a stream to the north, which they named Floyds River.

The death of Charles Floyd was the only death that occurred on the entire expedition to the Pacific coast and back, in spite of the near-starvation, disease and occasional Indian opposition the party faced.

MONUMENT TO A SOLDIER: The memorial at Sioux City, erected in honor of Sergeant Floyd.

SELECTED BIBLIOGRAPHY

Abbott, Newton Carl. *Montana in the Making*. Billings, Mont., Gazette Printing Co., 1939.

Allen, Paul. *Lewis and Clark's Travels*. New York, A. L. Fowle Co., 1900.

Anderson, Abraham C. *Trails of Early Idaho*. Caldwell, Idaho, Caxton Printers Ltd., 1940.

Anderson, Eva Greenslit. *Chief Seattle*. Caldwell, Idaho, Caxton Printers Ltd., 1943.

Arnold, E. Ross. *Indian Wars of Idaho*. Caldwell, Idaho, Caxton Printers Ltd., 1932.

Bailey, R. G. *River of No Return*. Privately published, 1935.

Bates, Colonel Charles Francis. *Custer's Indian Battles*. Privately published, 1936.

Brimlow, George F. *The Bannack Indian War of 1878*. Caldwell, Idaho, Caxton Printers Ltd, 1938.

Brown, Jennie Broughton. *Fort Hall on the Oregon Trail*. Caldwell, Idaho, Caxton Printers Ltd., 1932.

Burlingame, G. M. *John M. Bozeman*. Privately published, 1941.

  Montana Frontier. Helena, Montana, State Publishing Co., 1942.

Custer, Elizabeth B. *Boots and Saddles*. New York, Harper and Bros., 1898.

Defenbach, Byron. *Red Heroines of the Northwest*. Caldwell, Idaho, Caxton Printers Ltd., 1929.

Drury, Clifford Merrill. *Henry Harmon Spalding*. Caldwell, Idaho, Caxton Printers., 1936.

Dye, Eva Emery. *McLoughlin and Old Oregon*. New York, Wilson Erickson Inc., 1936.

Eells, Myron. *Marcus Whitman*. Seattle, Wash., Alice Harriman Co., 1909.

Federal Writers' Project. *Idaho Encyclopedia*. Caldwell, Idaho, Caxton Printers Ltd., 1938.

  Montana, a State Guide Book. New York, Hastings House, 1939.

  Oregon, End of the Trail. Portland, Ore., Binsford and Mort, 1941.

  The Oregon Trail. New York, Hastings House, 1939.

  Washington, a Guide to the Evergreen State. Portland, Oregon. Binsford and Mort, 1941.

Fougera, Katherine Gibson. *With Custer's Cavalry*. Caldwell, Idaho, Caxton Printers Ltd., 1940

Fuller, George W. *A History of the Pacific Northwest*. New York, Alfred A. Knopf, 1938.

Guie, Heister and L. V. McWhorter. *Adventures in Geyser Land*. Caldwell, Idaho, Caxton Printers Ltd., 1935.

Haines, Francis. *Red Eagles of the Northwest*. Portland, Ore., Scholastic Press, 1939.

Hawley, Robert Emmett. *Skqee Mus, or Pioneer Days on the Nooksack*. Bellingham, Wash., Miller and Sutherlen Printing Co., 1945.

Howard, Helen Addison and Dan McGrath. *War Chief Joseph*. Caldwell, Idaho, Caxton Printers Ltd., 1941.

Hunt, Frazier and Robert. *I Fought With Custer*. New York, Charles Scribner's Sons, 1947.

Irving, Washington. *Astoria*. New York, Belford Clarke and Co., 1836.

Kip, Lawrence. *Army Life on the Pacific*. New York, Redfield Publishing Co., 1859.

Langford, N. P. *Vigilante Days and Ways*. New York, Grosset and Dunlap, 1912.

Marquis, Thomas B. *A Warrior Who Fought Custer*. Minneapolis, Minn., The Midwest Co., 1931.

McWhorter, L. V. *Yellow Wolf; His Own Story*. Caldwell, Idaho, Caxton Printers Ltd., 1940.

Meany, Edmond S. *History of the State of Washington*. New York, Macmillan, 1946.

Miles, Nelson A. *The Personal Recollections of General Nelson A. Miles.* New York, The Werner Co., 1897.

Neihardt, John G. *Black Elk Speaks.* New York, William Morrow and Co., 1932.

Noyes, Al. *Dimsdale's Vigilantes of Montana.* Helena, Mont., State Publishing Co.

Parkman, Francis. *The Oregon Trail.* New York, Grosset and Dunlap, 1920.

Penrose, S. B. L. *At Waiilatpu.* Privately published.

Sandoz, Mari. *Crazy Horse.* New York, Alfred A. Knopf, 1945.

Sheridan, P. H. *Personal Memoirs of P. H. Sheridan.* New York, Charles L. Webster and Co., 1891.

Shiels, Archie W. *San Juan Islands.* Juneau, Alaska, Empire Printing Co., 1938.

Splawn, A. J. *Ka-Mi-Akin.* Portland, Ore., Binsford and Mort, 1944.

Splitstone, Fred John. *Orcas, Gem of the San Juans.* Sedro-Wooley, Wash., The Courier-Times Press, 1946.

Vancouver, Captain George. *Voyage of Discovery to the North Pacific Ocean and Round the World.* London, Robinson, 1798.

Vestal, Stanley. *Jim Bridger, Mountain Man.* New York, William Morrow and Co., 1946.

Wagner, Glendolin Damon. *Old Neutriment.* Boston, Mass., Ruth Hill, Publisher, 1934.

Walgamott, Charles Shirley. *Six Decades Back.* Caldwell, Idaho, Caxton Printers Ltd., 1936.

Washington State Historical Society. *Building a State.* Privately published, 1940.

Watt, Roberta Frye. *Four Wagons West.* Portland, Ore., Metropolitan Press, 1931.

Whiting, J. S. *Forts of the State of Washington.* Privately published, 1946.

Index

260

CHRONOLOGICAL INDEX

Students of history or others wishing to select a certain subject or period to read from beginning to end chronologically, may do so by reading the pages indicated below in the order in which they are listed.

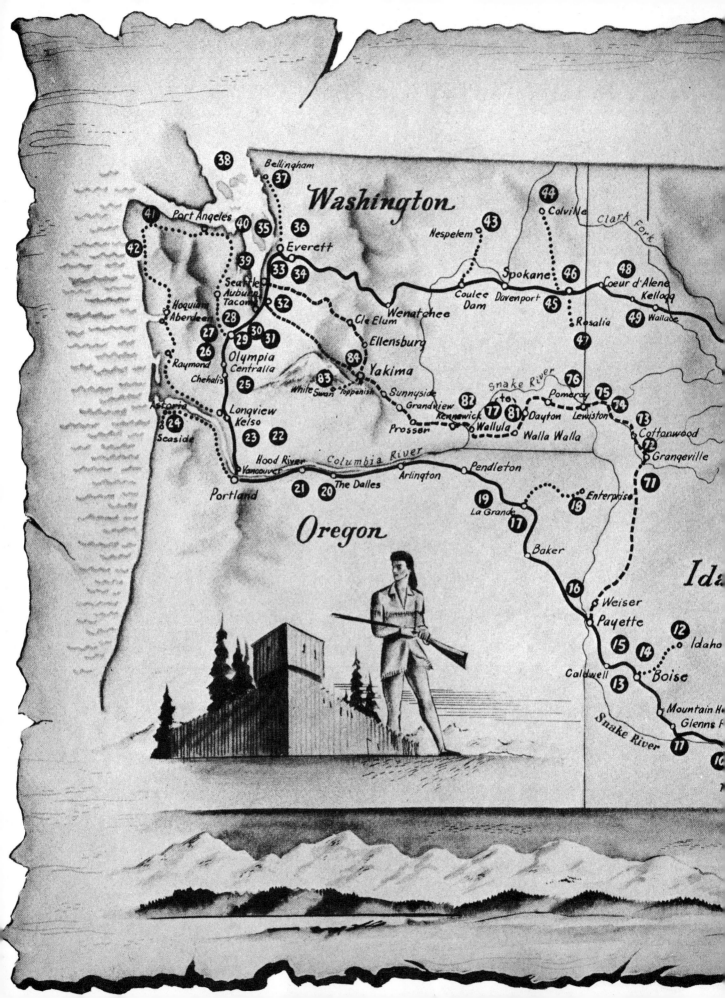

Montana

Missouri River

56 Havre

55

Great Falls

Missoula

Helena 54

Deer Lodge

Hamilton

Butte 63

Bozeman 66 Big Timber 67 Billings 68 70

64 65 Livingston

Big Hole

53

Dillon

57 58 59 62

Virginia City

Hardin

69

1 YELLOWSTONE
NATIONAL PARK

2

St. Anthony

3 Rexburg

Idaho Falls

Jackson

4 Blackfoot

6 Pocatello

7 American Falls

Soda Springs

5

Almo 8 9

Legend

—— Main Route
- - - Alternate Route
······ Side Trip
② Historical Marker